THOMAS PRADZYNSKI

MODERN REALIST

THOMAS PRADZYNSKI

MODERN REALIST

Catalogue Raisonné

AUGUST 1990 - MAY 1994

OLIVER CALDWELL AND SUSAN SNYDER
WITH RALPH MUSCO

CALDWELL-SNYDER PUBLISHING
SAN FRANCISCO

Published in the United States by Caldwell-Snyder Publishing
228 Grant Avenue, Fifth Floor, San Francisco, CA 94108 U.S.A.

FIRST EDITION 1993
Copyright ©1993 Caldwell-Snyder Publishing
Printed in Hong Kong through Asiaprint/Everbest

Library of Congress Catalog Card Number: 93-072847
Trade Edition: ISBN 1-884495-00-1
Collector's Edition I: ISBN 1-884495-01-X
Collector's Edition II: ISBN 1-884495-02-8
Collector's Edition III: ISBN 1-884495-03-6

BOOK & PRINT DISCLOSURE
Aside from the trade edition of 5,000 preliminary copies, there are three limited Collector's Editions.

COLLECTOR'S EDITION I, GALERIE DU MIDI

COLLECTOR'S EDITION II, LE BISTROT

COLLECTOR'S EDITION III, LIBRAIRIE ST. GERMAIN

Each Collector's Edition copy is signed by the artist and corresponds by number to its accompanied limited edition serigraph as follows:

Regular edition serigraphs printed on white Coventry Rag paper with 200 examples numbered 1/200 through 200/200; 5 artist's proof examples numbered 1/25 through 25/25; 3 printer's proof examples numbered 1/3 though 3/3.

Deluxe edition serigraphs printed on black Arches Cover paper with 150 examples numbered 1/150 through 150/150; 25 artist's proof examples numbered 1/25 through 25/25; 2 printer's proof examples numbered 1/2 though 2/2.

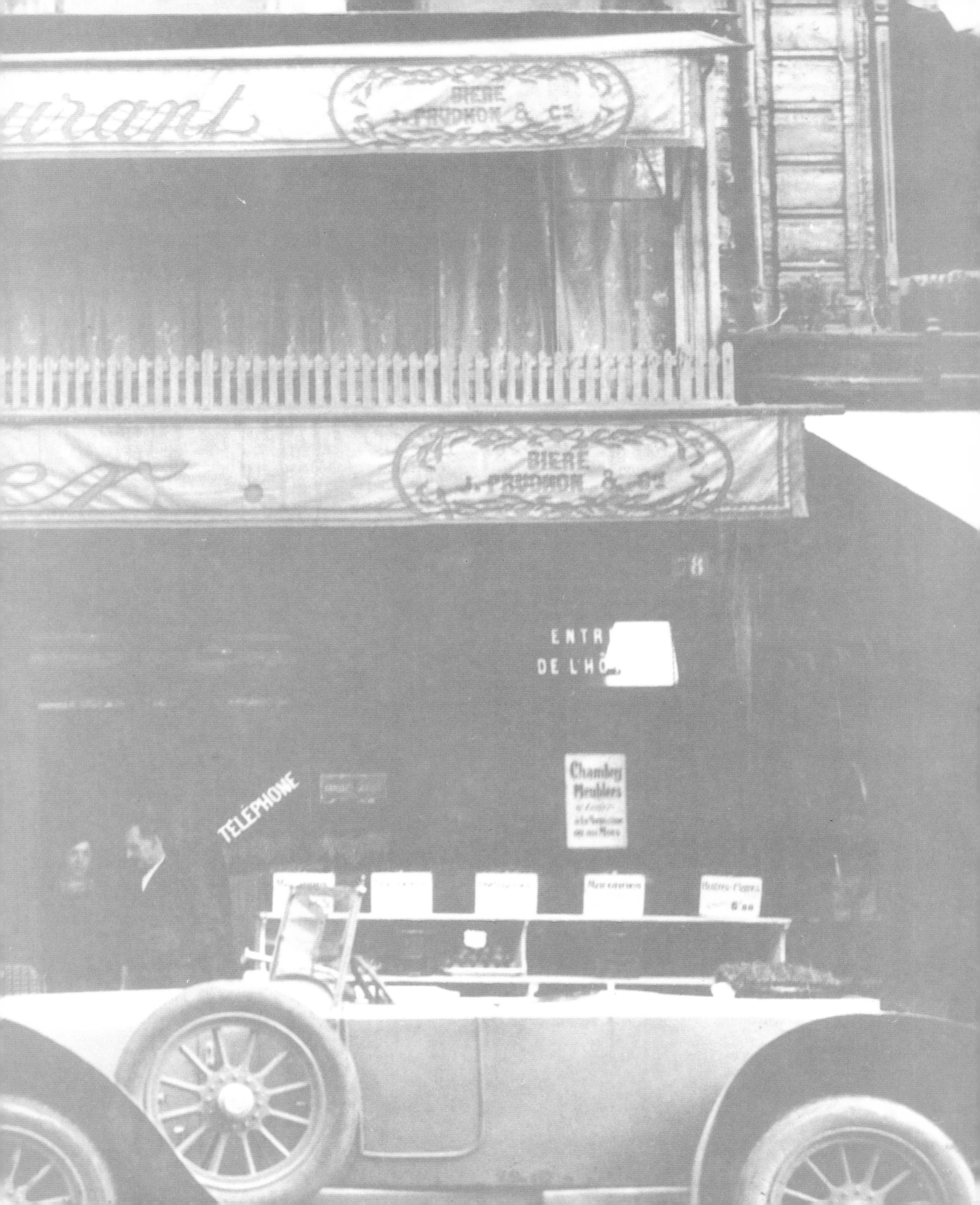

BIERE
BIERE
ENTR
DE L'HÔ
TÉLÉPHONE

ACKNOWLEDGEMENTS

We would like to express our warmest gratitude to all the friends and staff members of Caldwell-Snyder whose contributions and efforts have been invaluable to the artist's career as well as to the development of this book.

Our appreciation to the lineage of contributing writers and editors including, William Turner, Joseph Salinaro, Holly Willard, Debi Green and Joni Binder, whose contributory writings about the artist have been instrumental in the literary direction of this book.

Our thankfulness to Hiroo and Tomoko Hamano for their intuitive recognition of the artist's talents – which became the catalyst in launching the artist's career in Japan.

Our recognition to Gary and Sara Lichtenstein of SOMA Fine Art Press and Lev Moross and Bob Wolpert of Morosstudio, Inc. for their artistic excellence and craftsmanship in hand-printing Pradzynski's serigraphs.

Finally, our special thanks to Joanna Pradzynski for her faithful devotion and support of her husband.

Book Design:	Dag Madsen
Color:	Ampersand
Design Consultant:	Sergio Mello
Editor:	Ralph Musco
Production Coordinator:	Helen McNally
Personal Photography:	Tadeusz Kozakowski
Printing:	AsiaPrint/Everbest
Text:	Oliver Caldwell and Susan Snyder with Ralph Musco

Front Cover:	Passage du Lyon d'Or, acrylic, 45.5 x 35 inches.
Endpiece/Front:	Artisans du Marais, acrylic, 22.75 x 45.5 inches.
Endpiece/Back:	Passage du Cheval Blanc, acrylic, 18.5 x 41.5 inches.
Opposite Page:	Detail from Garage St. Antoine, acrylic, 25.5 x 39 inches.

TABLE OF CONTENTS

PREFACE

Preface

BY CHRISTOPHER D. KAMYSZEW, DIRECTOR OF THE SOCIETY FOR POLISH ARTS

Marc Chagall, one of many spirited artists from Eastern and Central Europe, said of his emigration to Paris, "It was because the sun of art shone at that time only in Paris . . . I thought that there was no revolution of the eye more remarkable than I witnessed after my arrival to Paris in 1910." Perhaps Thomas Pradzynski would speak similar words today, probably substituting "evolution" for "revolution", even though Paris' position as the capital of the art world may today be somewhat questionable.

The pilgrimage of Polish artists to Paris beginning in the early 19th century resulted in the most interesting episode of modern Polish art. A group of Polish artists associated with Ecole de Paris during the first decades of this century inspired three of the most sensational painters to escape from post-war Poland: Jan Lenica, Lebenstein, and Cieslewic. The work of these artists, which is now being rediscovered, became an embodiment of the vivacious spirit of the city—even for native Parisians.

But while Pradzynski's predecessors fled Poland in order to escape the country's traditional and increasingly limited artistic options for the developing media and styles available in other countries, Thomas left Poland to escape from its unrelenting cycle of bans and dictates which made artists unable to experience the freedoms of life, choice and creation. Pradzynski brought to Paris his melancholy, his longings and his personal mythology; combining these qualities with the revelations of acute realism and his adept use of modern techniques, he has given us some of the most charming and authentic expressions of our time.

The work of Thomas Pradzynski surprises us with endless mysteries and the similar nostalgic feeling we experience when looking through photographs in a family album. We also discover in his art a quiet familiarity, a sense of knowing, and a sense of history which roots us to our past. Though there are never any people in his canvases, he makes us feel no fear, only a wondrous timelessness with feelings of belonging and of comfort. His art gives us a sense of attachment to the world, a continuity that is confirmed by all details of a cityscape: open doors, cracked walls, half opened windows, a small white chair in front of a café. These symbols produce in us a feeling of steadiness and security, something of which we all dream . . . and it is because he touches us in this way that so many collectors bring his world into their homes, and into their lives.

Foreword

By Ralph Musco

We've all traveled, at one time or another, to a place that we hope never to forget. We return home, not only with a collection of memories, but with some physical record of our journey: a souvenir, a menu from a favorite restaurant, a special, meaningful photograph. As time passes, these memorabilia serve to refresh the fading images, to revitalize the washed-out colors, to somehow reverse the effects time has on our ability to remember. If we are fortunate, for even a single moment, we will experience the feeling Thomas Pradzynski injects into each painting he creates. Memories and emotions give life to his works - his souvenirs - translating them into hauntingly realistic images as precise as any photograph could be. Pradzynski has created a body of works centered about his adopted home, Paris, and, with the familiarity of a seasoned tour guide, leads the viewer on a private, romantic journey past quaint cafes and shops, down quiet sidestreets, undisturbed by local inhabitants or inquisitive tourists. The sights, the smells, the mood, the vivre, all present, all real and all felt.

Pradzynski orchestrates, in each of his compositions, a complex fusion of artistic skill and thoughtful, even loving, emotion for the city he so openly celebrates. The natural realism is not seen, but is rather felt, experienced, remembered. The consistency of shadow and variety of textures throughout each piece pinpoints the time of day, the weather, the season; elements that would distract the viewer are removed, explained visually in a terse but gentle manner, freeing the mind to become immersed in the passion of the scene. The feeling of the late morning sun or the slickness of the sidewalk in Caves de France is not imagined; it is an experience you have had, a memory already in your possession, relived on a quiet Parisian sidestreet.

Memories are among the most personal of possessions, secret notes kept on the experiences of a lifetime. Once lost, a memory is impossible to regain, to relive in the exact context of its original formation. Thomas Pradzynski, however, has preserved forever his own city of memories, open to visitors and unbridled by physical limitations, waiting to be shared and explored by the world. If you look closely, you will surely catch a glimpse of the most powerful element of his work, the thread that binds the artist to the art; each painting is a gateway, an open doorway to Thomas Pradzynski's soul.

Introduction

By Oliver Caldwell and Susan Snyder with Ralph Musco

Before now, it would have been difficult to write about the life of Thomas Pradzynski. Though there has been, for some time, a demand by collectors and gallerists, little information was available on the artist, certainly not enough to certify their intuitive regard for his importance, let alone form the foundation for an entire book on his life. With many artists, the desire to be a celebrity, to make a statement, to be a "person extraordinaire" will taint an interviewer's opinion; the artist may be portrayed as flamboyant or impulsive based on a single question-and-answer session when, in reality, neither adjective could be used to accurately describe his or her character. Thomas Pradzynski has been interviewed many times by journalists for art magazines, but, without an opportunity to become familiar with the man, the articles they produced failed to capture the substance of his work or, for that matter, his life. Combine the knowledge-gathering problem with the logistics involved when subject and author live on opposite sides of the world and the effort becomes more formidable. Another, more fundamental, problem kept this project beyond our reach. It is true that we could speak with Thomas and he with us, each struggling with the other's language, but it is not a simple task to reveal a feeling or personal ideology when you possess only a rudimentary knowledge of another person's language.

For the past eight years, we have had the good fortune to be his agents, to have become his friends and to thereby gain an insight to his feelings and thoughts. We have come to know what he really thinks about politics, social issues, life in general. He is a private man, cultivated, well-learned; a sincere gentleman possessed of refined European social graces. Thomas is not cut from the bolt of fabric used to create the insipid, flashy "Hollywood" genre of artists. There is no special mystique or hype about the man, only a genuine, concrete character, a character as solid as the aging Parisian walls that are his subjects. Our relationship with him has provided us with what we believe is a true picture of Thomas Pradzynski, and because of that, we have put pen to paper in an attempt to chronicle his life to date.

Often, the interest in reading a book such as this is not so much driven by a desire to study the technical aspects of an artist's work or the work's relationship to any contemporary dictum of aesthetic verification, but more to delve into the personal aspects of the artist's very existence. Who is he? What has he done and what is interesting about him? What is it that inspires the artist's vision, provides the courage to devote his entire

life to painting or sculpture or music? Ironically, if you ask Thomas this last question directly, he reveals his modesty, a trait that has always drawn people to him: "This dedication is a result of having, in all probability, a lack of ability to do anything else."

Never doubting his career choice or looking back on life as it could have been had he chosen a different path, Thomas has transmitted his personal expressions of life into his canvasses. He follows through with everything, never leaving a work unfinished due to dissatisfaction, not brooding over things he could have done differently in a particular painting; it is not uncommon for him to constantly revise the same boulangerie shop, for instance, until he — and he alone — is satisfied with the effort. Always open to suggestions and new ideas, he has not stagnated but instead continues to progress as

an artist. When we suggested that he paint on larger canvasses (he was used to creating very small compositions), the results were more amazing that we could have imagined. As the years passed, his mastery of style and unique reality gained increasing respect, but he did not need critical acknowledgment to keep his enthusiasm strong: that motivation is derived from within himself, his love of life and his work, his devotion to his subject.

It quickly becomes apparent that Thomas doesn't take life too seriously and

thus has not let his recent success influence his self-perspective. If anything, he underplays his success with friends and family so as to maintain a comfortable, friendly feeling, never making them feel uneasy. Underneath his peaceful demeanor lies an immediate sense of humor, manifested in playful gestures and an ever-present smile. With the certainty of his career and world-wide acceptance of his artwork, there has emerged a youthful spirit determined to hold on to the joys of life.

Amid the roar of the art market in the 1980's, there materialized a mandate to the market to standardize, to operate internationally, to conform to the modernist image. No matter where one traveled within the sphere of Western influence, you could find the standard selection of artworks by Andy Warhol, Joseph Beuys, Robert Raushenberg, Frank Stella, and others in similar standing. Thomas' art market, much smaller by comparison, had to be nurtured outside of this cultural imperium. We never felt the urgency to market his work among collectors intent on investing in the high-profile artists. These collectors speculated on the ever-increasing hype and price increases of the mega-superstar artists of the 80's, while Pradzynski's patrons bought his work out of pure appreciation for his artistry. They simply fell in love with his paintings, rarely considering the possibility for return on investment at resale. However, the speculative collectors — gamblers who likened their art investments to shares in the stock market — all but disappeared from the art scene, and with them went the inflated prices associated with contemporary super-artists.

The dissociation and independence from the hyper trends of the 80's have made it possible for Thomas' career to not only survive but to blossom in the retrenchment of the 90's. His art grows freely, unhampered by trendy critiques or auction results, flourishing in a somewhat private market. With a healthy disregard for trendiness or fads, those who collect his work are interested in its meaning rather than relative material value.

Publishers Susan Snyder and Oliver Caldwell with Joanna and Thomas Pradzynski in front of the wide spectrum of paints used in the creation of a serigraph.

An art dealer cannot invent an artist — he can only provide an audience and exposure of the art to prospective collectors. The tide of the art world rises and falls based solely on the artist, not on the merits of his support system. We have provided a greater audience for Thomas by traveling abroad — to Asia and to Europe — and by implementing a publishing program to market and distribute his graphic satisfy the insatiable network of collectors hungry for his work. We found that his art is almost universally accepted, fascinating people in India, Australia, Asia, Europe and South Africa, as well as here in the United States. Thomas' paintings do not possess a strict cultural context and therefore provide a readable quality understood equally well in all parts of the world.

Thomas is one of the few living painters whose work has resonance. This is undoubtedly due to the fact that he renders his paintings from a first-hand experience of his subjects: the streets of Paris. The artist is painting his home. Often, collectors inquire as to the location of a particular shop or café in one of Thomas' paintings so that they can visit the place when next they are in Paris. They want to go to the source of the inspiration, hoping to find something, like Elvis Presley fans visiting Graceland. Initially upon arriving at the location, there is the excitement of discovery, of having aligned the memory of the painting with its physical place in the real

Thomas Pradzynski with Tetsumi Minoh and Gary Lichtenstein of SOMA Fine Art Press.

works. With the introduction of serigraphs, many more galleries, and therefore many more collectors, are able to acquire Thomas' work. The demand has gotten so great, Thomas could never produce enough paintings to

world. Yet, the beauty of the painting is not an

exact reflection of a material structure; the

charm of the scene is taken out of context and

loses it associativity to the composition. It can

be compared to a movie idol: seeing an actor

portraying a suave debonair hero on the big

screen is never the same as meeting him in

person. The aura vanishes; the actor becomes a

man not much different than the movie-goers

who pay to see him perform. Likewise, the

aura of a Thomas Pradzynski Boulangerie

exists only in the painting, not in the French

bakery that bears a resemblance to it.

There is so much promotion and marketing involved in publicizing the identity of an artist's style that, once that style has become known, it becomes difficult for him to vary from the expected, to wander off and experiment with new ideas. The public along with the gallerists only want works that are true to the style associated with an artist and will not tolerate deviation beyond an acceptable limit; a dilemma arises when the artist feels he has to grow, to change, to express himself in a way in which he is truly sated. What makes Thomas' career special is that he has successfully satisfied the needs of the collector and the needs of the artist; his style is constantly maturing while his subject remains the same. Like George Braque, who did not venture away from the school of Cubism as Picasso did, but dedicated his life to solving its problems and perfecting its qualities, so too may we find Thomas unveiling ever new perspectives of his nostalgic Parisian streets.

Thomas Pradzynski with publishers Susan Snyder and Oliver Caldwell in Paris, October, 1990.

Portrait of the Artist

BY OLIVER CALDWELL AND SUSAN SNYDER WITH RALPH MUSCO

"When describing my art it is important to stress that I do not try to either imitate hyper-realism or tromp l 'oeil (deceive the eye). I attempt to romanticize the empty streets and the traces of the past and preserve places that are slowly disappearing. I am interested in detail and try to create an anecdote. I use light by manipulating reflections that come and go, and animating the beauty of a deserted street. I am fascinated with big cities like Paris and New York, and from their streets I try to find new visual realities for others to enjoy and discover. I love the past and present in every-day life and I hope to create that feeling in my art. At times I create a painting from a composition of several elements existing in different places, thus creating an image ideal to me. A lot of people see nostalgia in my paintings. It is a feeling I look for in places where life has stopped or is changing."

Thomas Pradzynski

Thomas Pradzynski was born in Lodz (pronounced "wooj"), Poland, on November 29, 1951. Several years earlier, in 1947, a Pro-Communist government was installed, and within a year of his birth, Poland adopted a Soviet-style constitution solidifying the rule of the USSR. Poland's recovery from the devastation and horrors of occupation was slow and thus provided a dismal environment in which to grow up. Still, Thomas exhibited, at an early age, a talent for art, which was influenced to a great extent by his aunt, Jolanta, who was at that time an artist in the city of Krakow. Jolanta, along with her husband, had become an artist between the World Wars, experimenting in Expressionism and other styles. She tutored Thomas, teaching him basic techniques, all the while helping him to develop an interest in art.

In 1960, his father, a representative of the Polish farm industry, was transferred to France. The family moved to the Montmartre district of Paris where Thomas, at the age of nine, was first exposed to the city that would later inspire and become his art. The excitement of the modern city was like no other he had experienced; Lodz, after all, was a dull, gray working-class town, a place to live without really living. Even as a small boy, Thomas recalls, he was taken by the spirit of Paris, the tempo, the culture, the vivre. In stark contrast to his native Poland, the city was a precious jewel, a wondrous toy, a fairy tale being played out for his enjoyment, and with the energy only the young can exert, he experienced it. He also

became enamored of the freedom expressed by its inhabitants, was totally absorbed in it; perhaps most importantly, he was captivated by the Parisian street painters, the effulgent hues that gave life to their canvasses exciting him, leaving an indelible mark on his psyche. Like a siren, Paris had seduced another stranger, stolen another heart, taken one more prisoner. Though the young artist would escape temporarily, he would return — like so many artists before — and he would stay.

The elder Pradzynski's business finished, he returned his family to Poland in 1965, and Thomas, now 14, resumed his artistic studies, concentrating on drawing and painting. His homeland was a world away from Paris, both ideologically and culturally. While the West was enjoying the progressive atmosphere of the 60's, Poland was still struggling to free herself from the unwelcome influence of the Soviet Union; the Iron Curtain, now just a bad memory for most, was then an impassable obstacle, a formidable edifice of stifling oppression, a constant reminder of the stranglehold exercised by Moscow. But even the strongest barrier couldn't suppress the energy of Poland's teenagers, couldn't thwart their uncontrollable desire to join in the new Renaissance occurring outside the Communist Bloc. Sharing the same values as their peers in New York, London, and, of course, Paris, Thomas and his contemporaries were able to procure, via a thriving black market, the very symbols of Western irreverence: rock 'n' roll records, junk food and Levi's jeans. The price was high — even higher should one be caught with this contraband — but well worth it to hear Bob Dylan's early songs of revolution and the heart-felt blues of Eric Clapton. Pradzynski recalls that there was a strong desire among Poland's youth to display the same unrestricted attitude as was occurring in the West, but it wasn't always possible: "I was a hippie. I lived with my girlfriend, we had long hair, music, marijuana, the same as in the States, but it was different. We wanted to be independent, to be on our own, but there was

Le Pas Perdu

ACRYLIC ON CANVAS
89 x 117 CM. / 35.5 x 47 IN.
SIGNED: LOWER RIGHT
SEPTEMBER 1992

Le Petit Journal

ACRYLIC ON CANVAS
100 X 65 CM. / 40 X 26 IN.
SIGNED: LOWER RIGHT
OCTOBER 1992

no place for teenagers to live, no apartments. That was part of the system." But the void created in Thomas' heart when his family left France could not be filled by these mere glimpses of the world outside Lodz. A poor substitute for its Western European counterpart, Poland lacked the rich, contemporary culture of music, theater and political expression the young artist had come to admire in Paris. He would find a way to return, but for the present, it was not meant to be.

Thomas continued his studies in art, and in 1968, after graduating from Lycée Française in Warsaw, he spent two years in private drawing studies at Academia Szutk Pieknych, also in Warsaw. Still, Thomas had aspirations of becoming an artist, but success would require more than desire; while it was true he had a love of art, Poland, under the watchful, repressive rule of Soviet Russia, was not the best place in which to be an artist. Says Pradzynski, "In a country like Poland, you don't make many plans. It's one of the characteristics of communist life that it curbs individuality and dreams and projects." Leaving home to live with his girlfriend, Joanna — the woman who would eventually become his wife — Pradzynski set out to enjoy the "new" world, to express his individuality and pursue his art, but this would end shortly after the death of his father in 1968. Due to an obligation to his widowed mother and other societal considerations, Thomas' mildly rebellious interlude with the 60's was replaced by more practical endeavors. A bright, intelligent young man, Pradzynski entered into Social and Economic Sciences Studies at SGPIS, Warsaw, graduating in 1976 with Master's degrees in both Sociology and Economics. Thomas still yearned, however, to be an artist and did not look forward to the drudgery of pursuing either of his major fields as a career. He decided to continue his education, this time studying architecture and art at Ecole Politecnique, Warsaw. Pradzynski admits that he had a keen interest in buildings, their structure, their textures, but he never completed his studies. Becoming bored by the

technical aspects of architecture, he continued to paint, taking several art courses during his tenure at Ecole Politecnique. He was making money selling paintings, earning a decent living copying icons and producing original compositions. A building in Lodz, a local child, a street scene; Thomas painted them all, always trying to develop a style that satisfied him, that would help him to become successful. The thought of painting for a living overcame him; Thomas, at the age of 26, concentrated his energies on art.

Comfortable with his potential to earn a living, Thomas and Joanna married in 1976. They settled down to life in an apartment in Lodz, each pursuing their own career. Pradzynski continued to paint and sell work, each sale propelling him forward; "It's a great feeling when someone buys your work; it's as if they're saying, 'good job'." In 1977, having saved enough for a short vacation, Thomas and Joanna decided to visit Paris. He had never

forgotten Paris and had told Joanna the stories of his youth; he had cherished memories of Paris, its beauty, its ambiance, and he wanted her to experience the West for herself.

It was as if he had never left. In an instant, he was a child again, this time sharing his playground with a new friend. Together they strolled the streets and boulevards, explored the Latin Quarter and Montmartre; new experiences for Joanna and a rebirth for

Thomas. They drank in the beauty of the city and became intoxicated with it, a temporary departure from reality and the sobering atmosphere of their home. So excited, so enraptured were they by this place that they decided to extend their vacation, carelessly letting their visas expire. "When you are living in the center of the universe," quips Pradzynski, "why would you want to leave?" Returning to Poland with an expired visa would certainly preclude any chance of obtaining another, so, with no notice to family or friends, Thomas and Joanna left Poland behind for good and embraced their new life together in Paris.

Thomas immersed himself in his art, continually striving to perfect his style and develop his technique. He made extensive studies of light and texture, transforming the labyrinthine streets of the old city into his personal outdoor studio. He began to paint naive street scenes, capturing the form, the colors, the textures of the aging shops and stuccoed façades. Never influenced by any one artist's style or technique, Thomas tried to learn something from all that he observed, looking for elements he could incorporate into his own technique. At the same time, he was growing ever fonder of the city itself, becoming quite Parisian, adopting it as his home. Paris holds a secret that only artists know, some mysterious conundrum revealed only to the gifted; Thomas discovered that secret. Like so many before him, his artistic abilities matured and flourished in the City of Lights. For him, this force manifested itself in open windows, quiet courtyards, empty streets; he became concerned that these venues were quickly vanishing. Having already had success selling his works to local galleries, he began to compose works of overpowering detail, paintings so real that they surpassed reality. Pradzynski set out to "romanticize the empty streets and the traces of the past, and to preserve places that are slowly disappearing." Sometime in the early 1980's, urban realism became his trademark, not born out of a necessity for uniqueness, but out of a deep-

Pradzynski's work. On this particularly cold winter's day in January 1985, Caldwell and his cousin, Walter Fischer, were walking through Paris, touring the local shops and galleries, reveling in the surroundings that had served as home to the likes of Picasso and Gertrude Stein. They happened across a group exhibition featuring local artists, and decided to have a look, the purpose of Caldwell's trip being to find new works for the San Francisco-based gallery jointly owned by Susan Snyder and himself.

Exhibitions of this type are a normal occurrence in Paris; Henri Rousseau first showed his work at a similar event in 1886 and was, almost overnight, propelled to the top of his field. So it isn't surprising that they simultaneously stopped, gazes fixed upon a most unusual and simple little painting of a dark blue Parisian shop with a door the same color red as a fire engine. Standing alone, this little gem of a painting — the canvas measured 8 inches by 12 inches — sparkled with color, apparently orphaned by its creator, the only

seeded, altruistic emotion; the art he created not only echoed his surroundings, but also communicated his passion for their preservation.

His compositions were immediately successful. He began to exhibit his paintings in local galleries, selling enough to provide a stable income for his wife and himself. It was at one of these local shows that Oliver Caldwell first became acquainted with offering of its kind in the gallery. The painting was so radiantly clean, so illuminated with color that it gave the impression of an abstract work, the subject simply portrayed in the reduced and primal elements of the great works of that genre. The use of crisp, basic colors and depth of field, reminiscent of a Mondrian canvas, was captivating. Caldwell and his cousin frantically searched the painting for a name, finally finding traces of a signature that appeared to say only 'Thomas'. It wouldn't be an easy task, in a city as large as Paris, to locate a person even if one had a complete name to go on, but to attempt such a search with only a Christian name — a common Christian name at that — was nothing short of impossible, a time-consuming folly bordering on an act of utter lunacy. But, in the instance he had first observed Pradzynski's work, Caldwell knew that he had to find the artist responsible for so magnificent a composition. Finding a painting of such beauty at an obscure exhibition of local artists was, by itself, not a significant accomplishment; more

Le Fenêtre No. 35

ACRYLIC ON CANVAS
53 X 37.5 CM. / 21 X 15 IN.
SIGNED: LOWER RIGHT
AUGUST 1990

Rio Di S. Polo

ACRYLIC ON CANVAS
80 X 117 CM. / 32 X 47 IN.
SIGNED: LOWER LEFT
NOVEMBER 1989

deny the existence of the piece, trying to dissuade them from paying any attention to the tiny painting that had obviously been abandoned by its owner. Certainly, an artist of any worth would stand by to represent his work, so why would anyone be interested in such an unimportant painting as this? But the two were interested, very interested, and, unfortunately, in spite of all their inquiries, they were still without the artist's name. They would have surely given up if the pair of travelers hadn't been approached by a friend of Thomas', who said that it was possible to arrange a meeting with the artist directly.

amazing was that no other artist, no other patron of the exhibit could, or more likely would, help to identify its painter. Numerous attempts to cajole their way past the jealousy of the other artists in attendance failed, and they held out little hope that this avenue of inquiry would yield the painter's identity. No helpful information was forthcoming; most of the participants not only denied any knowledge of the artist, some went as far as to

Several days after first seeing the diminutive canvas entitled Rue du Norvins, Caldwell was introduced to Thomas at his home in Montmarte. He reviewed several other works that Thomas had at his residence, and after discussing prices and sizes, purchased three paintings. Pradzynski was to prepare the works for shipping and deliver them to Caldwell's hotel the following day.

Paintings in hand, Thomas,

accompanied by his wife, arrived at the Hotel-de-Florence near Boulevard Haussmann, a meeting which Caldwell remembers well. "We spoke for some time, and I was taken by the couple's determination to succeed, to survive in a place not originally their own, totally resolved to overcome the changes their lives were subject to." Meeting these two young people, displaced — albeit by choice — from their home, Oliver was instantly fond of them and, though the similarity was subtle, he felt

that their reasons for coming to Paris were allied in their characteristics. Thomas and Joanna had come to Paris to find something: she to experience a part of Thomas' past, he to find a path to his future. This gallery owner from San Francisco, too, had come to Paris to find something, the object of his search not nostalgic or inspirational, but nonetheless a prize that his great city could surely produce: works of art. Caldwell had chosen Paris for its reputation as the center of the art world, some

Le Vieux Bistrot

ACRYLIC ON CANVAS
37.5 X 53 CM. / 15 X 21 IN.
SIGNED: LOWER RIGHT
MAY 1993

sort of magical department store, its shelves stocked with treasures ready for the taking.

Returning home, Caldwell hung the little red door painting in his office at his gallery in San Francisco. He was surprised by the number of clients who would ask for the price of that painting, the Parisian shop with a bright, red door, usually during negotiations concerning other artworks on hand at the gallery. The usual response was that it was a souvenir of a trip to Paris and that it was,

unfortunately, not for sale. As time went by, the offers for that painting became more and more enticing, almost embarrassingly high, and Caldwell began to secretly wonder what all of these people saw in that canvas. The reason for the attraction soon became a moot issue: collectors wanted this work, and were willing to pay for it. While sentiment is a noble gesture, Caldwell came to the realization that this little painting didn't belong to the past, shouldn't be a memento hung on a wall as a nostalgic reminder of a trip once taken. It was obvious that it represented the future, his future, his partner Susan Snyder's future, and of course, Thomas Pradzynski's future. Finally a client made an offer on Rue du Norvins that was so immense, Snyder and Caldwell could not refuse it. Sure that it was a sound business move — the influx of capital was a necessity — they accepted the client's offer and immediately invested the profits in a round-trip plane ticket to Paris.

Caldwell found Thomas once again at his home in Montmartre and ebulliently related the events leading to this second trip to Paris. He explained to Pradzynski the great interest the gallery's clients had taken in his work and the artist, his dream of success fast becoming a reality, quickly joined in Caldwell's enthusiasm. They discussed delivery schedules, sizes, commissions; a new experience for Thomas, a gamble for the pair of under-capitalized gallery owners. Was the initial interest a fluke, a one-time mass hysteria that would never again occur? Or had they found the elusive needle in the proverbial haystack, a jewel so rare that the world would jump at a chance to possess it? Caldwell left Paris, this time not with a souvenir for his office, but with a dream of great things to come.

Caldwell and Snyder, excited by the initial response to Thomas' work, decided to take an enormous risk: a one-man show — their first one-man show for a totally unknown artist. They reasoned that, if one tiny painting could attract so much interest — more interest than had been demonstrated on some of the better-known artists that were represented - the show would naturally be a landmark success, not only for the gallery but for Thomas as well. It was not the type of business decision they teach one to make in school; it was totally instinctive, downright foolish, and absolutely necessary.

They didn't have much time to consider the consequences of losing that last dollar. Arrangements had to be made, literature had to be printed, clients had to be invited. The small gallery's staff was too busy with all the preparations to wonder if they would have a job the day after the show. It soon became apparent that they lacked the one thing needed most for this show: space. There was ample room to display the paintings; there was no room to accommodate the clients and necessary libations. A tent was erected in the yard adjoining the gallery, hopefully sufficient in size to oblige the guests who had been invited. All the necessary trappings in place, they had only to wait for the invitees to come and buy up every Pradzynski in the gallery.

And come they did. A large portion of the guests were regular attendees of art auctions, always on the look-out for a bargain and not likely to ever buy a painting at retail, but Caldwell and Snyder were cautiously confident that the work would inspire them to break with tradition and indulge. They watched, almost in horror, as the abundant quantities of food and champagne that had been provided disappeared nearly as quickly as their hopes for a successful show. These ravenous art gallery groupies had made quick

work of the buffet, pausing just long enough — between mouthfuls of cheese and copious swallows of champagne — to rave about the paintings, not one of which had yet been purchased. Caldwell became discouraged, resigning himself to the fact that he and his partner had spent every last dime on what was turning into a farewell party for their gallery. As the opening evening wore on, however, a most unusual conspiracy became obvious. After devouring the hors d'oeuvres, these money-conscious bargain-hunters had collectively plotted to buy each and every painting in the show. It was an unbelievable event, a unanimous showing of overwhelming approval by the most discriminating group of collectors ever assembled in one location. The reason for this interest in Pradzynski's work suddenly became crystal clear: the general perception of Thomas' work was that it was remarkable work at a fair price, more valuable than the price tag revealed. Negotiations were minimal, haggling unnecessary; the prices were fair. These collectors were content to take home a charming, nostalgic rendering of Paris, knowing in their hearts that the investment was a good one.

The show was scheduled to last a week, but didn't make it that long: the gallery ran out of paintings. Such a success was it that Caldwell immediately contacted Thomas, intent on purchasing every piece of work the artist could produce. The two partners had already talked of holding an annual show of Thomas' work at the gallery, as well as a plan to market his work elsewhere. They were, however, apprehensive about promoting the artist to other galleries in the U.S.; the diversity of regional taste in a country this big was unpredictable, and many areas were already saturated with "hot" artists and successful graphic programs. For years the two had heard much of the accessibility of the Japanese art market. In fact, they had sold numerous Pradzynski paintings to Japanese tourists at the gallery in San Francisco; they had come to Caldwell-Snyder and now Caldwell-Snyder would go to them. Japan, it was decided, would be a good place to sell the artist's work; Snyder and Caldwell set out to lay siege to this vast, new market. Thomas Pradzynski would be introduced to the world and Caldwell-Snyder would serve as his promoter. Thomas would paint, Snyder and Caldwell would sell, and all would live happily ever after — or so they hoped.

The apparent popularity of Thomas' work in Japan was encouraging, and the owners of Caldwell-Snyder became increasingly confident, so much that they decided to

*Makoto and Izumi Kato, Hiroo Hamano, Thomas Pradzynski and
Oliver Caldwell at Kato Studio, 1990.*

*Collectors Dr. Yohei Hashimoto and Mrs. Hiroko Hashimoto with
Thomas Pradzynski.*

participate in the Tokyo Art Expo scheduled
for March 1990. The show was the first of its
kind in Japan, an international event that
attracted the world's top galleries — Leo
Castelli, Isy Brachot, Fujii Gallery. Surrounded
by these "giants" of the industry, Caldwell and
his partner were a bit intimidated, but,
nonetheless, quite successful — by the second
day of the show, they had sold every painting.
Several of the paintings were acquired by
Hiroo Hamano, a fine art executive for Mitsui
Corporation; this highly diversified company
later became the exclusive distributor of
Thomas' work in Japan. Through the
dedicated and enthusiastic efforts of Hiroo
Hamano, Mitsui Corporation had, in a span of
two years, organized numerous exhibitions in
galleries and department stores, including
Odakyu Department Store, Daiwu
Department Store, and Takashimaya
Department Store. Mr. Hamano subsequently
ventured further into the art industry when he
founded Tokyo International Fine Art (TIFA),
an art company which today is the exclusive

promoter of Pradzynski's work in Japan.

The success experienced at Tokyo Art Expo bolstered their confidence further, and the two purveyors of things artistic had no doubt that it was time to expose Thomas Pradzynski's art in America. This introduction came at the Los Angeles Art Expo in October of 1990. Demand for the artist's work was increasing faster than Thomas could produce paintings; Caldwell and Snyder bridged this shortfall by publishing limited edition serigraphs. The first of these serigraphs, entitled Leonora and Les Memoires de Paris Suite, were made available to art dealers from all over the country at Los Angeles Art Expo; these were quickly consumed by avid collectors, at a time when the art market was becoming flat.

Demand for Thomas' work was now greater than ever, and all indications pointed to continued growth. It had been four years since the one-man show at Caldwell-Snyder, long enough to discredit any beliefs that this might just be a fad, a short-lived flight of fancy

Hiroo and Tomoko Hamano with Thomas Pradzynski and Oliver Caldwell at the Golden Pavilion in Kyoto, Japan.

Thomas Pradzynski and Oliver Caldwell with collectors Mr. and Mrs. Yamamoto and Mr. Tanabe of the Odakyu Department Store.

Susan Snyder, Oliver Caldwell and Thomas Pradzynski with founder of TIFA, Hiroo Hamano, and his wife Tomoko at N.Y. Expo, 1993.

Susan Snyder Thomas Pradzynski and Associate Director, Debi Green, celebrate the signing of "Leonora", the first limited edition serigraph.

destined to end as abruptly as it had begun. Caldwell-Snyder's owners began 1991 with the Tokyo International Art Show, returning to the city that had been anxious for the opportunity to purchase Thomas' art. Their expectations were again high, and, at the opening party, celebrated in advance what was sure to be another strong showing in Japan. No one, unfortunately, had anticipated that the Vernissage (gala preview) would coincide with the bombing of Baghdad and the start of Desert Storm. Concern turned to the Gulf and events unfolding there; the show became secondary, the general mood somber. The initial excitement was pre-empted by the sobering news of war, and the three — Hamano, Caldwell and Snyder — couldn't help but think that the show was ruined. As if the bombs were actually landing in Tokyo, the success of most dealers in attendance was destroyed. Pradzynski's success, however, was miraculously unaffected by the hostilities in Iraq; collectors and dealers patronized the booth and bought nearly all Thomas' works on the first day of the show. While all around dealers were having trouble just attracting prospective customers, the team of Hamano and Caldwell-Snyder had managed to sell a substantial number of paintings; they agreed amongst themselves, somewhat jokingly, that the Pradzynski market was "bomb proof."

They ended 1991 where it had started — in Japan. Thomas was becoming quite the celebrity throughout Japan, and Caldwell-Snyder took advantage of this by embarking on a two-week tour of department stores and galleries in different cities. Interviewed by television and newspaper journalists at every sojourn, the tour resembled a modern "whistle stop" campaign, the old-fashioned caboose being replaced by the sleek bullet-style trains used extensively in Japan. It was like a real-life rags-to-riches story; there were actually Pradzynski "groupies" following them around, young girls asking for autographs and photos, as if Thomas were an actor or a rock star.

Thomas did his best to remain unchanged despite the attention he had

Gallerists Tom Barnes and Michael Rochard with Oliver Caldwell at the Thomas Charles Gallery in Las Vegas.

Susan Snyder, Thomas and Joanna Pradzynski, and Oliver Caldwell in San Francisco. Memorial Day, 1993.

Lev Moross, Bob Wolpert, and Oliver Caldwell at Morosstudio, Inc.

received in Japan. He adopted a rigorous work ethic to meet the increasing demand for his work. During the day, he painted in the streets and in his studio for hours on end; at night, he would relax among his friends — mostly other artists — haunting the cafés, sometimes into the next morning. There was a camaraderie among these artists, but there also existed an underlying fear that one of them might break free of the pack, overcome the common status of relative anonymity and become famous abroad. In their collective lack of acclaim was a kind of strength, the group together self-reinforcing; it was a precarious symbiosis successful only through the absence of individual success. Thomas, sensitive to this relationship, hid his growing fame from his companions, not through selfishness but out of concern for their feelings. The struggle for gallery recognition was grueling indeed; he had triumphed, they had not, and he felt it best that they not know the magnitude of his growing success. He enjoyed the company of his friends, felt comfortable in their presence,

and he knew that the envy would destroy the mutual respect they had for each other.

Determined not to allow his fame to compromise the friendships that were so important to him, Thomas chose to live in a modest fashion, maintaining a lifestyle uncluttered by the trappings of fame. To do otherwise would surely emulate a kind of bragging, and that would definitely not do. While they could certainly afford more, Thomas and his wife continued to live as they always had, extravagant furnishings and techno-toys exchanged for humble surroundings and warm relationships. Their home, sparsely decorated yet comfortable, hid Thomas' new-found recognition from all but their closest acquaintances. Even the most mundane of creature comforts associated with modest success are curiously absent, even today.

His conviction to simple living is evidenced not only in the way he lives in Paris, but also in his habits away from home. There is no desire to impress anyone by superficial means — fancy clothes, big cars, extravagant accommodations. He dresses comfortably, and when Thomas visits Caldwell-Snyder in San Francisco (about once every six to eight weeks), he brings only a small carry-on bag. He seeks modest accommodations in a local hotel, and, but for his indulgence in fine food, portrays to the world his modesty.

Thomas' art continues to have a strong following, in markets from Tokyo to Chicago, New York to Hong Kong, accepted world-wide not only for its quality, but its value. His art is represented by over 100 galleries, and is shown regularly in international art fairs. The Polish Museum in Chicago features Pradzynski's work in its annual ArtFest Exhibition, a showcase for selected contemporary Polish artists. Every painting includes a small piece of his soul, a personal view of the world he so loves, expressed with the energy of the youth. Despite his good fortune, he doesn't take life too seriously, nor has he lost his perspective.

Le Chocolatier

ACRYLIC ON CANVAS
27 X 20 CM. / 11 X 8 IN.
SIGNED: LOWER LEFT
MAY 1993

He is outwardly at peace with himself and everything around him: his wife, his friends, his work, his life. A keen sense of humor often surfaces, another manifestation of the man's total love of life, and the child-like, playful spirit he possesses.

The changes which occurred in his native Poland during the 80's have made it possible for Thomas and his wife to re-establish ties with friends and family in their former home. Thomas takes advantage of this by periodically making a nearly 800-mile drive

to visit his mother. Often, mother accompanies son to his home in Paris, where they spend time together, a luxury that became possible only after Poland opened her borders to travelers. In the past, following his self-imposed exile to Paris, he would on occasion visit his mother, crossing the border with a French passport. These visits were special to his family, brief reunions that never really lasted long enough. Struggling to survive in an economy wrought with graft, waste, and corruption, his relatives would insist, always against Thomas' will, to treat him to dinner in the finest restaurant in town. That meal would easily cost the equivalent of a full month's wages, but it didn't seem to matter; Thomas' visits were a reason to celebrate, to be extravagant. Thomas, ever grateful for the treatment he received, thanked them, hoping someday that he would be allowed to reciprocate, knowing it would never be permitted. A meal in the simplest Parisian cafe was far superior to the fare served in even the most famous of Poland's restaurants, and yet these poor, working class people thought nothing of the expense; Thomas saw this comparison as a reflection of his life in microcosm, a metaphor that succinctly described his reasons for quitting Poland for France without regard for the sacrifices involved. Pradzynski has no desire to return permanently to Lodz, for, as the artist says, "Paris is my home." He is at present unconcerned with the politics of his birthplace, but recalls his interest during the Solidarity-inspired strikes in Gdansk in the summer of 1980: "It was a very exciting time, but it has become boring. I'm just not interested anymore."

Thomas continues to excel as an artist, constantly working to develop his skills and his style, looking not so much to the future, but to preserving the pieces of the past he finds so exciting. Though his reputation continues to grow, and will undoubtedly continue as the art market in general recovers from the leaner period of the 90's, he still doesn't like to make too many plans. He just wants to paint.

Pradzynski's Aesthetics

By Oliver Caldwell and Susan Snyder with Ralph Musco

Many art critics, historians and collectors want to classify an artist's work into one of a seemingly unending list of accepted definitions. Impressionism, Expressionism, Primitivism, Realism, Cubism, Any-and-Everyism, on and on ad infinitum, covering an enormous diversity of styles practiced by an equally enormous number of artists. Entire bodies of scholarly works exist which distinguish the aspects of a style, place it historically, analyze it psychologically, define it exactly and totally. In the rare instance when an artist has broken the bonds of classical definition, another chapter of history begins, a new style is born, a new ism added to the list.

Upon analysis, it becomes apparent that Thomas Pradzynski's work cannot be defined by any one term, cannot be restricted by the boundaries imposed by a word. While his work has been called Realism, Super-Realism, Photo Realism, Primitivism, Naivism, it is none of these while at the same time it includes elements of them all. So, it seems that a fresh, new term must be introduced: Modern Urban Realism. The only way to understand its definition is to experience the mysterious phenomenon that is Thomas Pradzynski's work.

The street scenes portrayed in Pradzynski's paintings appear to be within the general category of Realism; the definition of Realism, however, is as varied as the individual. Historically, it is accepted that present-day Realism originated in a movement dominant primarily in France in the mid- to late-19th century, a movement led by and identified with the works of Gustave Courbet. In the tradition of 16th century Italian painter Michelangelo Merisi da Caravaggio and 17th-century Spanish painter Diego Velasquez, Courbet painted that which he saw, influenced by the political and social upheaval prevalent at the time. He believed that "painting is an essentially concrete art, and can consist only of the representation of things both real and existing." Although Pradzynski maintains close tradition with Courbet in style, a conflict exists; Courbet asserted that, "I hold the artists of one century basically incapable of reproducing the aspect of a past or future century." While painting the present, Pradzynski paints the past. A nostalgic dream-like presence in each of his works links the two, making them inseparable.

Thematically, his work is more closely related to Edouard Manet, whose interpretation of the form was a fusion of Realism in technique with Myth in subject matter. While the individual elements of the artist's street scenes do exist, Pradzynski's painted buildings are not entirely

La Mere Catherine

ACRYLIC ON CANVAS
80 X 40 CM. / 32 X 16 IN.
SIGNED: LOWER LEFT
MARCH 1987

(PREVIOUS PAGE)

true to their location within the Parisian cityscape, and in their assemblage become fictional. Manet's definition of Realism would still include Pradzynski's work, as his idealized arrangement of subject matter is portrayed in the life-like manner associated with the genre. While Pradzynski is not the first to meld fact and fantasy — this theme of "fictitious realism" found its way into the 20th century and onto the canvasses of other contemporary artists — his work is distinctive because it contains a deep, psychological introspection that elevates it from mere reportage to the level of inspired visual poetry.

His early works were greatly influenced by the Parisian street painters he witnessed during his youth. As a child he was captivated with the color, the detail, the apparent realism portrayed on their canvasses. The untrained street painters practiced a naive style characterized by an overabundance of meaningless, unnecessary detail. All subjects in this style of painting tend to be treated with the same amount of detail; bricks portrayed in background structures, for example, receive the same attention as do those forming a building in the foreground. Another prominent feature of this style is a distorted perspective, the relative size of objects and figures determined by psychological interest without regard to natural proportions. Summarily, the most unassuming of subjects becomes lost in a complicated obfuscation of visual banality.

During 1977, Thomas was faced with a dilemma as to how he should handle the urban scenes, whether to make them more naive or more realistic. Constantly, he was beseeched by collectors to fortify his paintings with more objects, more detail; in short, to return to naive art. Many of his contemporaries were developing styles that led them away from the early primitive genre; the style had become restrictive, the artists' realized perceptions were being reduced to something child-like, the aura of their subjects obscured by triviality. Some succumbed to the temptation of hyper-realistic detail; the charming quality of their paintings replaced by

Via Della Colonna

ACRYLIC ON CANVAS
71 X 106 CM. / 28 X 42 IN.
SIGNED: LOWER LEFT
JANUARY 1990

Monte Carmela

ACRYLIC ON CANVAS
40 X 80 CM. / 16 X 32 IN.
SIGNED: LOWER RIGHT
NOVEMBER 1989

the slick, unfeeling blandness of illustration. Others relied on the aesthetic strength of their works, opting to paint familiar locations — the Sacre Coeur or Cafe de Fleur — in hope that some collector, enamored with a particular landmark, would purchase these works in spite of the inherent flaws of the style. Still others remained true to the naive style and practiced in the tradition of street painters before them, with a slight twist: they stationed themselves at locations most likely to be frequented by tourists, selling their paintings to travelers ready to bring home a custom-made souvenir of a trip to France. This struggle over whether to pursue a naive or a realistic style gave birth to a new method of presenting his subjects. Thomas turned away from both and pursued a more personal interpretation of his subjects. He was very concerned with the whimsical trappings of the Naive style and the cold illustrative Realism. Thomas has distanced himself from that influence while still maintaining his devotion to both moieties. It is very easy to take the simple and make it complex; it requires a much more skilled effort to make the complex simple and understandable. During the late 1970s, Thomas painted larger perspective scenes of Paris as in the scope of the Naive artists. Slowly, however, he began reducing the postcard expansiveness of the scenes to more close-up vignettes of buildings and doors. This was the beginning of one of the most important changes in his work; a change that has become central to much of his painting through the '80s and '90s.

At one point, Thomas painted works that were small in size, yet still comprised of the same concentration of detail. The diminutive scale, he felt, was vital to the intimacy and he thus resisted working in large format. His switch to larger formats resulted from a demand from American collectors; homes in the United States are bigger than their European counterparts and Pradzynski's tiny gems became almost invisible when situated in such oversized quarters. Changing the scale of his work created new problems, and Thomas was very hesitant. As the size of the image changed he noticed that the emphasis within the image shifted and new solutions would have to be found in order to retain the aesthetic sensibilities. Certain elements were naturally predominant at one size, while at another size these features became less accented.

The realistic detail present in Pradzynski's paintings reveals the vulnerability of his subject's exterior surfaces, the unrelenting effects of weather, use and time. Equally important is a representation of solidity, of structure, an assurance of permanence. This is part reality and part imaginary, for Pradzynski is deeply concerned with the inevitable extinction of these aging edifices and, through his tools — brush, canvas, paint — he attempts to preserve each for future generations to visit and to enjoy, if not physically then visually. Each building embodies its own dignity and traditionalism, exuding a powerful yet humble endurance toward the unflappable effects of time.

The planning of modern day Paris is attributed to the foresight of Baron Georges Haussmann, prefect to Napoleon III in the mid-19th Century. Haussmann had a vision of the future and drew up plans for a great metropolis which Napoleon commissioned him to effect during the years 1853 to 1870. Haussmann positioned the main streets and boulevards as long, straight thoroughfares focusing on the major traffic circles, intersections, and architectural landmarks of the city. Narrow, winding streets connected his major highways, where the inhabitants of Paris established their unique homes, shops and neighborhoods. Haussmann's imagination gave birth to the City of Light. His place in history is secured by the successful implementation of his own idea of what Paris would someday become.

Today, Paris is being rebuilt. The roads are the same, the landmarks still intact, the Seine still splitting the city into two equally beautiful sectors. But the shops and cafés, boulangeries and patisseries are being reconstructed, products of a new vision, a new imagery of what this great place will one day become. Thomas Pradzynski has successfully laid claim to a re-imagined Paris, one completely his own. Its streets are empty but the complex symphony of human experience still resonates in the doorways and courtyards. His city is a unique configuration of reality, dreams and remembrances, of mystery and anticipation; he has transformed the alleyways, cafés and open doorways into metaphor. Pradzynski's Paris is nothing less than haunting, an evocative streetmap of our own emotions and perceptions.

Currently, Thomas Pradzynski's work has gained world-wide acceptance, a popularity due, at least in part, to the accessibility of his imagery. It is universally appealing, not only for its careful treatment of the subject, but also for the intricacies of the

Cours Des Halles

ACRYLIC ON CANVAS
60 x 45 CM. / 24 x 18 IN.
SIGNED: LOWER LEFT
JANUARY 1991

Nicolas

ACRYLIC ON CANVAS
65 X 100 CM. / 26 X 40 IN.
SIGNED: LOWER RIGHT
JULY 1990

artist's style. Pradzynski's message is at once readable, yet so psychologically and emotionally complex that no simple interpretation is fitting or rewarding. An amateur viewer is immediately captured by the familiar, charming, intimate quality of Pradzynski's city vignettes and is likely to describe these works as photographic or life-like, missing completely the underlying abstraction of the compositions; these viewers nonetheless find the paintings enjoyable, pleasing to the eye and skillfully executed. But through his use of light and suggestion of detail, he has transcended the hard-edged structural boundaries of traditional and contemporary Realism. Herein lies the key to the power of these works, overwhelmingly rich with feeling and mystery; everything is real yet nothing is real. Each piece embodies the artist's unique view of the world he portrays, combining fact and fantasy, almost challenging the viewer to look closer for clues and signs of his nonconformity. These non-existent edifices, constructed from myriad memories and images accessible only to Pradzynski, are actually puzzles with multiple solutions. The reality of the scene is totally interpretive, and each viewer's interpretation is as unique as his or her own memories and experiences.

Nostalgia pervades Pradzynski's work. It is as much an element as the buildings, the alleyways, the courtyards that occupy each composition. Without it, his paintings would be as devoid of life as the streets he portrays, the elegance of the works reduced to splashes of color forming nothing more than a picture of some dilapidated storefront recorded for posterity only to prove it had once existed. It

is a feeling for which he searches in the deserted streets, a mood he discovers in an image reflected off a window or in a building's crumbling façade. The presence of this nostalgic idealism — a dedication to the preservation of these magnificent old buildings — draws the viewer into the scene, whispers a message into his ear, makes him feel what Pradzynski feels. Whether it is the empty street, a riderless bicycle propped against a wall, an unattended table in a small café, his images urge us to hold tight our links with the past, cherish them for eternity. But his imagery speaks in double entendre; the metaphorical, almost playful inclusion of open windows and partially-seen courtyards lead us from the past into an unknown future, inevitable yet mysterious, time not yet expended but destined to one day slip by. It is as if he is challenging us to remember bygone experiences but also to live for things to come, to love what we've done as much as what we are about to do, are doing now; to go and build a new cache of memories, capture them and

Alimentation Generale

ACRYLIC ON CANVAS
117 X 89 CM. / 47 X 35.5 IN.
SIGNED: LOWER RIGHT
DECEMBER 1991

add them to an ever-expanding library of sentimental recollections.

In Fenetre No. 73, the walls are painted with very expressive, loosely-defined stokes which create an almost ethereal lack of detail, a treatment much more suited to the portrayal of some far-off celestial body than the well-defined, rigid structure of a wall. But yet it is immediately apparent that this enigmatic vertical surface defines the plane on which is set the central element of the painting. Likewise, the plants occupying the windowsill are portrayed in a similar manner, lacking the intricate detail of the central subject, yet expressing the completeness of form through a mixture of color and shape. The leaves are depicted much as one would show sunlight reflecting on still water, appearing to be totally disconnected from the stems and twigs that they populate, shimmering, floating on the surface of the painting like abstract pieces of green confetti tossed from some point beyond the field of view, pausing in space just long enough to provide the illusion of foliage. This is an elementary technique of Pradzynski's, a deliberate subversion of the realism associated with common, everyday objects that grants the freedom of a secondary motif, allowing the suggestion of expected details while minimizing them in the impressionistic sense. He avoids the banal trappings of naive style by understating that which is obvious, enticing the viewer to fill in the missing pieces as his imagination sees fit.

Another facet of Pradzynski's style is his use of the abstract to represent reality. He paints elements in ways that cause them only to pretend to be what they seem, but are in fact unique unto themselves. Take, for example, the fiery, orange color of the wall in Fenetre No. 73. This particular hue would, in photographic replications, suggest the oxidation of iron by air and rain, but Pradzynski has dramatized the color to act as an emotional intensifier, accentuating the mystery and beauty of the darkened window. In this way, the choice of color goes far beyond

Les Deux Fenêtres

ACRYLIC ON CANVAS
40 X 53 CM. / 16 X 21 IN.
SIGNED: LOWER LEFT
JULY 1990

the precise indicator of rust perpetrated by the forces of the natural world; it defines an individual, almost separate phenomenon, an independent character that mixes with the scene and radiates its own, undeniable presence. By itself, it would distract the viewer from the unknown world beyond the

window. However, Pradzynski adds a strong cool gray wash to the painting to somewhat subdue the fiery force of the orange wall and re-focus the viewer to the drama that is sure to unfold beyond the enigmatic portal. The window is open; a mental passage takes place and we are transported from the world outside to an unknown arena. An immediate feeling of warmth, of familiarity, of hospitality is conveyed by the potted plants perched on the sill. There is no fear, no apprehension about that which lurks in the unexplored reaches beyond the open window; the recently tended vegetation suggests that a friendly denizen awaits our arrival, perhaps to chat about time gone by and share a glass of wine.

Abstract shapes formed by stucco upon the building's stone surface in Une Bicyclette a Florence create the layered appearance of antiquity, a style comparable to that of earlier Realists like Maurice Utrillo. Having studied architecture for several years, Pradzynski is intimately familiar with the materials of construction and how a given architectural elements texture will react to light and weather, as well as the likely interaction of one element with another. Pradzynski's architectural forms, while remaining classic in design, create mysterious shadows, secret passageways. The effect of light is allegorical as well as natural: the

Au Relais

ACRYLIC ON CANVAS
80 x 60 CM. / 32 x 24 IN.
SIGNED: LOWER LEFT
JUNE 1991

shadows provide a feeling of depth and contour, while at the same time romantically embracing the scene and preserving its intrinsic detail.

This masterful use of light and shadow further acts to convey a feeling of perpetuity that can best be analyzed in Twilight on Rue de Madiran. Illumination from several sources converges on the scene from different angles, and, reflecting from the damp streets and weathered facades, creates multiple perspectives. Thus, light seems to have a symbolic connotation that transmutes the piece into a prismatic collage of time itself, applied with a sensitivity that renders a subdued ambiance while simultaneously enhancing the elements of expectation. As realist Richard Chiriani describes his aquatic subject matter's form through light and shadow, Pradzynski's wandering shadows compliment robust detail with abstract shapes to take the viewer's imagination inside the quiet buildings.

Thomas Pradzynski paints from first-hand experience. He begins each morning with a walk from his home in the Montmarte district to the nearby cafés for coffee and pastries. Along the way, he passes boulangeries, patisseries, cordonneries, wine shops, all built in the late 19th and early 20th centuries. The colorful storefronts and textured walls are not just part of the scenery but are his models, life-size inhabitants of his massive outdoor studio, a studio that covers the width and breadth of Paris itself. And as he strolls past these locales, he greets them, takes solace in their existence, feels the life emanating from each of his subjects; they are no less alive to him than were the models that posed in the studios of Matisse and Rodin. Thomas, through his intimate contact with these quaint, rapidly vanishing Parisian structures, has been immersed in their aura, bonded to them, witnessed their grand scale; their shared experiences cannot be replicated from photographic studies alone. A city, any city — be it Paris, New York, Peking — is not flat; it does not exist in two-dimensional space.

Lucien Agan

ACRYLIC ON CANVAS
80 X 60 CM. / 32 X 24 IN.
SIGNED: LOWER LEFT
APRIL 1988

Au Gardon d'Argent

ACRYLIC ON CANVAS
89 X 117 CM. / 35.5 X 47 IN.
SIGNED: LOWER LEFT
SEPTEMBER 1991

It is, therefore, impossible to represent in a medium that allows only height and width. Painting strictly from photographs fosters a dullness, a blatant disregard for the reality of life; this sickness pervades much of contemporary painting. To emulate an Utrillo or Vlaminck from a book and expect to capture the atmosphere of Paris is an absurdity: there could be no color, light, sound, air. Pradzynski shares life with the

Le Massif Central

ACRYLIC ON CANVAS
60 X 45 CM. / 24 X 18 IN.
SIGNED: LOWER LEFT
MAY 1991

subjects of his work, not in the abstract sense, but in a very real way: Paris is where he lives and breathes. He also shares with Paris an integral component of his overall mental attitude towards life: he is a Parisian. Far from simple architectural renderings, each painting is a personal anecdote, a brief sagacity painted instead of spoken. His work reveals a deep emotional bond with the world, imbued with a polymorphous quality absent from much of contemporary art. Even three dimensions are too little for Pradzynski; he includes a fourth, more esoteric plane in his work, a stratum inhabited not by the physical but by the spiritual.

Thomas does use photographs as a secondary reference but he never settles on a subject captured in the camera's lens; he creates one, as surely as he creates the painting that contains it. While memory and sentiency guide the artist's composition, photographic references serve only to show visual detail: direction of illumination, density of shadow, and other such factual aspects.

These details are apt to fade from memory over time, so the artist doesn't waste effort on their retention; Pradzynski uses his mind's eye on the more important task of preserving the feeling of his find. After framing in his lens the pictorial essence of the subject, he takes numerous pictures; later, Thomas uses his reference photos to concoct a scene, to recreate the architectural positioning of his imaginary structures. With delightful artistic license he sometimes combines a boulangerie from one street with a grand passageway from another, creating a composite, aesthetic force greater in value than the sum of its parts. The effect is for the work to slow up the eye of the viewer, to encourage him or her to forego the quick look and opt for a more unhurried absorption of Pradzynski's heartfelt images.

In recent times — that is, post-World War II — contemporary art institutions have moved away from the arduous task of teaching painting and sculptural skills to their charges, surrendering to new, more esoteric concepts. The practice of making things and developing

Porte 28 Uzes

ACRYLIC ON CANVAS
27 X 22 CM. / 11 X 9 IN.
SIGNED: LOWER RIGHT
JULY 1991

Baldini

ACRYLIC ON CANVAS
45 X 106 CM. / 18 X 42 IN.
SIGNED: LOWER LEFT
NOVEMBER 1989

skills was slowly replaced by an increased accent on deep-thinking, the contemplation of art psychology, history and strategy. It was a more noble endeavor to analyze the nature of art than to practice the manual conveyances necessary to achieve a sense of artistic accomplishment. The teaching of disciplined skill, focusing on drawing from the living model and natural motif, has nearly been denounced; this facet of the process is, perhaps unjustly, criticized as being a hostile influence on creativity. The rudiments of art

are overlooked, neglected, replaced with the notion of self-expression without regard for technique. The popular tide flowed toward a more abstract and conceptual goal; the teacher's views were transferred to a seemingly endless stream of hungry minds, mutating them, transforming them into an army of cloned artists. Student became teacher, emulating style and creativity, all the while fueling the selfish, insatiable egos of their journeyman instructors. This is not to say that the establishment destroyed the fabric of art itself, that there was a universal adherence to this new set of artistic commandments; there were those self-reliant artists, Thomas among them, who continued to refine their individual styles through perseverance and dedication.

It is painful to imagine the repercussions if such a malignancy were to infect other artistic disciplines; could one find an accomplished pianist who avoided practicing, repetitively and incessantly rehearsing, for countless thousands of hours, immeasurable harmonic scales, arpeggios, and finally complete scores? Fortunately, Thomas was not influenced by contemporary academia. At an early age, he developed, under the tutelage of his Aunt Jolanta, formal drawing skills and an understanding of the principles of art. Thus, by concentrating on the basics of his vocation, Pradzynski's creativity emerged as a manifestation of his independence and self-discipline, augmented by the proficiency with which he plied his trade; his is a more traditional creativity, unconcerned with the approval of the academics.

Eventually, the decreased emphasis on the use of real-world subjects led to a heavy reliance on photographic reproductions. The convenience afforded by modern film developing techniques enable the student to obtain an instant subject, ready to be reproduced in all of its lifeless splendor. Obviously, it is more convenient for an art student attending classes in downtown New York to copy a Monet painting from a 35 millimeter slide than it is to fly to the South of France and paint landscapes. The works produced in this way are dimensionally limited and nothing more than realistic portrayals of flat objects, lacking depth and emotion; a sensuous nude transformed into a naked body, a vibrant landscape turned into a hand-painted picture postcard, so much inconsequential non-art being pawned off on an unwary, maybe even uncaring, commonality.

There is a paucity of skilled realist artists who execute their works from a personal perspective, relying more on first-

Vieil Immeuble
Rue du Baigneur

ACRYLIC ON CANVAS
40 X 53 CM. / 16 X 21 IN.
SIGNED: LOWER LEFT
DECEMBER 1991

civilization have been greatly influenced by the presence of movies and television. We, along with our children, parents, even grandparents, have grown-up bathed in the light of the moving picture. The flickering images pass by at a rate too fast for our eyes to capture any single one; we have no alternative but to be manipulated by the overall effect. Technological advances have eliminated the need for the viewer to use imagination; the camera can trick us into believing we are in outer space or living in another era in history or floating among white blood cells inside the human body. Reality exists in short bursts of activity timed to coincide with commercials and news briefs. The pervasive power of mass media has permeated every facet of our society and culture, even art. It has proclaimed itself as art and has thereby become a new source of anxiety for artists.

The values of mass media are diametrically opposed to those of painting and sculpture. Presented in a rapidly flowing, seemingly endless stream, its raw unfiltered

hand experience and intimacy with their subjects than on synthesized content. These select few realize the difficulty involved in simulating a feeling of familiarity, fabricating emotion in the absence of real knowledge. Their compositions are possessed of an inimitable quality, a subtle editorial on life itself that cannot be copied from still images; the photo captures form but lacks essential, purely emotional, details that fail to survive reproduction.

The last few generations of Western

data flashes before our eyes. It is visible yet unseen, not allowing the luxury of a long attenuated look. Images pass, a constant current that cannot be slowed — save through the intervention of video recording equipment — or contemplated in real-time. Unlike works of art, these are not physical objects, they possess no density, occupy no space; they are not real. It is impossible to touch these phantasms, to set them before us and examine them at our leisure. Do they possess meaning beyond that presented in the plot, innuendo unsuspected in the well-rehearsed dialogue, messages hidden by the director? Contemplation of the form is not allowed, nor will it be tolerated.

Art is different from that; it lingers. Visit an art museum, a gallery, an exhibition; the very fact that art can be visited, like a relative or friend, heralds its desire to be seen and studied, possessed, loved. It can easily be contemplated, analyzed, enjoyed again and again, the limit on such endeavors imposed by the individual and not by the medium. The messages transmitted by works of art are not limited by the constraints of time, nor are they subject to the approval of sponsors or advertisers; they are not cancelled if the ratings fall, nor are they changed to suit the perceived tastes of the consumer. Pradzynski goes beyond this idealistic interpretation in that his work occupies not only the physical domain but also communicates a spiritual meaning; an in-depth interpretation of its contents combines the experience and emotion of both viewer and artist.

The abstractness of institutional art teaching combined with the predominance of mass media has produced a fine arts movement given over to information and not experience. A new breed of artists is being created; they have been force-fed massive quantities of raw, unassimilated data and not been given any concrete guidance with which to apply that information to art. While many living artists tend to paint introspective and conceptual works, canvasses rich with suggestive imagery but lacking in technical

La Chambre Bleue

ACRYLIC ON CANVAS
80 X 117 CM. / 32 X 47 IN.
SIGNED: LOWER RIGHT
DECEMBER 1991

skill, most exhibit the shallow quality associated with heavy dependence on mass media. Substance has been replaced by style, and the fabric of the imaginative process has been left in a weakened state.

Uncrippled by contemporary hype, Pradzynski's work maintains a deep sense of moral dignity and reverent appreciation for the city he loves. More profoundly, he has shaken the bonds of commercial patronage and remained true to his own goal of preserving these endangered Parisian venues. He has not allowed himself to be influenced by television, to become impeded by any short-sighted conceptualism which could mutate his paintings into architectural renderings. Nor does he want to become more significant than his work, an iconoclastic spectacle more involved in himself than in his art. He is an artist in the classic sense; his skillful use of fundamental elements projects him light-years beyond his contemporaries. Far removed from the droll practitioners of visual trickery, those whose best attempts appear on posters sold at flea markets or included with the purchase of a picture frame, Pradzynski could in no way be considered an illustrator; illustrators merely reproduce fact, while Pradzynski has the unique ability to create it. His work resonates with the inspired rhythm of a life enjoyed, that enjoyment transferred from the artist's hand to the canvas, a breath that animates the scene and invites the viewer to join in his celebration of being.

Often, Pradzynski creates an entire vista rather than a centralized scene, allowing the viewer to explore not only the immediate urban environment, but also the less frequented venues visible in these compositions. By carefully controlling his use of vanishing point and perspective, Pradzynski orchestrates a rhythmic transition between multiple elements. In Le Café, for example, a dark, intimate passage lures the viewer to visit

Le Divan Blanc

ACRYLIC ON CANVAS
32.5 X 22 CM. / 13 X 9 IN.
SIGNED: LOWER RIGHT
FEBRUARY 1989

a private inner garden of sunlit trees, an option just as interesting and curious as the colorful storefronts occupying the foreground.

With rigorous yet playful precision, Thomas engenders in his creations a personal interpretation of urban isolation, showcasing a particular feature while maintaining a constant interest and uniformity of integration. Noteworthy is the method by which he diverts attention from the non-essential, perhaps distracting, nuances of his scenes; he provides

Le Maraichin Café Bar

ACRYLIC ON CANVAS
40 X 80 CM. / 16 X 32 IN.
SIGNED: LOWER LEFT
DECEMBER 1990

us with as much or as little detail as we need to deduce such things as weather and season. When we walk on wet pavement, we understand that it has rained; if we see snow, we do not have be told that it is winter. That is not to say that these elements are trivialized; they are treated with immense sublimation. It is important for Pradzynski, to set the perfect stage, to fabricate before his audience everything needed to enjoy a walk through his beloved Paris. He doesn't want you to waste time wondering whether you'll need an umbrella; instead, he wants you to feel the rain, or the warmth of the sun, or the biting teeth of winter. His patient, lucid development of subject yields in his work a richness, a density of meaning that draws us deeper into the world created by and for Thomas Pradzynski, a world that he graciously allows us to share.

The soberness of Pradzynski's style relies on the use of single brush marks to enunciate form. There is a poetic consistency in his style that lends the air of expectancy, a theatrical quality; like intricately detailed sets, Pradzynski compositions seem to have just been vacated by actors. Sometimes a chair or bicycle is posed, lit as though by a director, unoccupied for the moment but soon to be reclaimed by its owner.

One becomes increasingly aware of the importance of short, straight-line accents to the overall configuration of the work. The vertical and horizontal features of architectural elements (i.e., doors, window sills, pipes, awnings, metal gratings, blocked wall surfaces, etc.) augment the awareness of a linear sub-structure; the lines counter each other and are not primarily perceived as such except in acute analysis. This nearly invisible network of supporting detail is part of a deliberate technique used by Pradzynski to organize his work. However, its construction is more intuitive than premeditated; sharp accents

along with the frequent use of light and dark contrast keep the work taut and visually aggressive. Sometimes the monotony of the repetitive straight lines is disrupted by a curvilinear object — the rounded back of a chair or bowed surface of an awning — to achieve a rhythmic flow and accentuate the feeling of depth.

There is the tendency to compare artwork with the new standards imposed upon the physical properties of photography and its seizure of perspective and color. A viewer's immediate perception of Thomas' work is highly influenced by the recent permeation of contemporary photography and mass media. Sometimes the knee-jerk reaction to describe his work is to call it "like a photograph."

But unlike architectural photography, Pradzynski's art is transcendental, taking the viewer from his existing stance and providing a place to explore and experience another world. A world sometimes rich in nostalgic feelings and memories of Paris once visited, or a world unmechanical and built in scale to man without monstrous glass, steel and concrete skyscrapers. There is an immediacy of purpose, a presence, an almost palpable sensory experience to these compositions that transports one to Paris' sidestreet attractions. The works are simple, but in their simplicity beckon the viewer to read each carefully and completely.

The network of vertical and horizontal linear elements is essential not only in structure and composition, but also in understanding Thomas' approach to painting. Thomas does not allow the visual elements to lapse into a condition where texture plays a primary role. Such a lapse would make the work too soft and too romantic for the artist's intent.

Thomas tries to achieve a delicate balance between the toy-like quality of his subjects and the more definitive classical Realism. These subjects, though initially appearing to be real, are uniquely simplified to achieve maximum visual presence and avoid a softness of static realism.

Today there is a high degree of certainty about his work and himself. The work is more assured and polished, with a different kind of force— somewhat less austere, more seductive, and with a painterly light. Thomas is part of the broad and diverse world of realist painters, dealing less with the real world than with a re-imagined real world.

Instead, Thomas' unique style is that of asymmetrical composition and contrasting definition of the various subjects. Each individual part of the painting — a chair, a wall, a window — is heightened by juxtaposed and contrasting elements that may be under-painted or simplified. Some parts of the paintings move toward impressionist softness while other parts have a stately hard-edge beauty. All elements in Thomas' paintings are not competing for identity because each element is not painted with the same intensity of color and light. There is a rhythm of high and low painterly treatment that allows the viewer to see a poetic balance. In Hyper-Realism and Naive art, all subjects and

Batignani-Florence

ACRYLIC ON CANVAS
80 x 100 CM. / 32 x 40 IN.
SIGNED: LOWER LEFT
NOVEMBER 1989

Kendall and Company

ACRYLIC ON CANVAS
51 X 80 CM. / 20 X 32 IN.
SIGNED: LOWER RIGHT
NOVEMBER 1989

perspectives are in equal force and detail and thus are in constant competition.

Although one is tempted to react first to the work with a sense of nostalgia, one quickly realizes that this is not the emotional key with which to unlock meaning and beauty. The Realist artists discover that their external reality is inescapable from their own subjectivity. The depiction of a scene is primarily interpreted by the artist and secondarily interpreted by the viewer. Through this dual interpretation, the artist is able to achieve a shared experience from an otherwise personal environment. As a Realist,

Pradzynski focuses his compositions on the amount of content he can add to the subject matter. In order to reveal more than one would ordinarily see with the naked eye, Pradzynski utilizes his talents of "photo realism." The canvas ultimately contains more subject matter than the eye would normally perceive, therefore taking the perspective of a camera. Details in the painting provide the viewer with a sense of intimacy by bringing the subject within the range of public scrutiny.

Pradzynski's work, though highly associated to Hopper in subject, is more aligned to Hopper's influences than to Hopper directly. Both artists are influenced by Manet who developed in his compositions of walls, roads and sky, an emptiness with emphatic blocks of shadow and wide, flat planes of unfastidious, reverberant light.

Similar to the hushed mood of Pradzynski's street scenes, Edward Hopper's still cross-sections of city life portray a mood suspended in time. Both artists use similar

La Chaise Blanche

ACRYLIC ON CANVAS
71 X 100 CM. / 28 X 40 IN.
SIGNED: LOWER RIGHT
APRIL 1991

Passage Benaiad

ACRYLIC ON CANVAS
40 X 27 CM. / 16 X 11 IN .
SIGNED: LOWER RIGHT
MAY 1993

forms of Realism to record a memory of relevance in their own lives. The similarity of content in their street scenes is notable: vacant streets, open windows, and the warmly lit presence of inhabitants within decorated store fronts. In Pradzynski's paintings, Paris is viewed in perspectives that are devoid of people. This requires one to place himself at the scene and to explore an inner reaction; a technique also used by Hopper. The space created between the viewer and the scene in Pradzynski's paintings allows a pedestrian perspective to develop. Although their portrayals are of separate cities, the Realistic method complimented by a somber mood are threads common in both the paintings of Thomas Pradzynski and Edward Hopper.

The obvious absence of the human form adds an extra dimension to the realism of the work. This addition of life by its omission heightens the viewer's anticipation, increases the feeling of intimacy with the scene. It is almost a foregone conclusion that someone will soon occupy the white chair in Le Café,

and the bicycle in Une Bicyclette a Florence. In a seemingly static environment, these objects take on life of their own; catalysts capable of initiating action at any moment, provoking the feeling that someone may occupy the chair or ride away on the bicycle. Metaphorically, they act as a human presence, an abstraction of Pradzynski's own persona.

Pradzynski reconciles us with the world, not by protest, irony or political metaphors, but by the ecstatic contemplation of an imagined paradise. Repeatedly, he offers us a glimpse of his mindscape, a place where we can come and go as we please, to move unimpeded by the restrictions of the physical world. It is not like any locale we are likely to visit on Earth or anywhere else.

It is in Thomas Pradzynski's works, in his Paris, that the past is reborn, the world revitalized; it is here where even imperfections are perfect. When we see through his eyes, when we are the viewer on the other side of his canvas, we live in his world, and our world is changed forever.

ATELIER PEINTURE
1re PORTE DROITE SOUS LA VOUTE
COUR du BEL-AIR
56
HUGNET

Paris, City of Light

BY OLIVER CALDWELL AND SUSAN SNYDER WITH RALPH MUSCO

First settled between 250 and 200 B.C. by members of the Parisii tribe, Paris has a rich historical past. Some of the most famous and beautiful structures in the world grace this city of over 2 million people, including the Eiffel Tower, the Arc de Triomphe, the Tuilleries Gardens, the Cathedral of Notre Dame, the Sacre-Coeur Basillica, and, of course, the Louvre. Throughout history, her riches have been plundered, her people subjected to the ravages of war. She has been occupied by foreign armies no less than three times, first by Julius Caesar in 52 B.C., again during the Franco-Prussian War in 1871, and a third time by the Nazis from 1940 to 1944. During three revolutions (1789, 1830, and 1848), she was the sight of unrest and bloodshed. In 1968, confrontation again visited her in the form of student rioting. Yet, in sharp contrast — almost in disregard — to the violence evident in her historical record, Paris has served, during the whole of the 19th century and fully half of the twentieth, as a beacon for artistic expression unequaled by any, past or present. Artists from all over Europe and the United States — indeed, the world — have been inexorably drawn to this creative Mecca. Writers, painters, musicians and poets, like moths to a flame, they come to this place, seeking something, some key, some inspiration to further evolve their abilities of individual artistic statement. It is odd that many of the artists who live there are not native Parisians or even French citizens. They have come to be among their contemporaries, to live in the center of the world as they believe it to be, as many before them believed it to be. Most have taken refuge in small communities like Montmartre and Montparnasse, among their own kind, to share in the dream of living freely as artists; to indulge in a lifestyle as eccentric or subdued as they deem necessary to enhance their creativity; to support themselves through the patronage of tourists and local benefactors alike. Some have come to refine their talents, some to experiment with new styles and techniques. A few among them have already found fame while others search for the right combination of skill, technique and subject to perhaps attract a following and a steady income.

But why Paris? Why not Brussels, Rome, London, New York? Is it the people, the spirited, rebellious inhabitants of this cultured metropolis that appeal to artists? Maybe it is the architecture, the spectacular landmarks that lure them there? Could it be the city's heritage, its place in the historical record? There is no single answer, just the simple realities that artists are as much a part of Paris as the Seine, and that Paris is as much a

Cour du Bel-Air

ACRYLIC ON CANVAS
40 X 32.5 CM. / 16 X 13 IN.
SIGNED: LOWER RIGHT
MAY 1993

(PREVIOUS PAGE)

Femmes a une terasse de café, Paris, 1925.

Café Restaurant Pasquier, Paris, 1914.

part of art as the painters, the sculptors, the writers and the musicians who flock to her. To compile a roster of the great artists whose essential ideas took shape in Paris is to survey names that have changed the course of art and thinking since the end of the Age of Enlightenment: Delacroix, Manet, Renoir, Hugo, Zola, Monet, Toulouse-Lautrec, Degas, Soutine, Cezanne, Picasso, Braque, Utrillo, Vlaminck, Matisse, Camus, Sartre. Yet, the enormity of this city's contribution to art is not realized until an attempt is made to limit the list. Can we omit Rodin and Balzac, Debussy and Rimbaud, Van Gogh and Gaughin? Do we

Le Café Restaurant, Paris, 1914.

forget Gertrude Stein and Ernest Hemingway, or F. Scott Fitzgerald, or Edward Hopper, all giants of American art and literature, upon whom Paris made an indelible impression? How many others sat in her dark cafés amidst the thick smoke of Gitanes, consuming copious amounts of wine and coffee, engaging in debate, each searching for an individualized vehicle with which to pursue their own artistic nirvana?

In fact, our notion of Paris is inextricably tied to the artists and writers who made the city their subject as well as their studio. Toulouse-Lautrec, perhaps more than any other turn-of-the-century artist, painted the straight unvarnished truth of the city and made its denizens his subject, forever capturing the characters and personalities that roamed the streets, bars and brothels, his brush bristled in acid. Utrillo and Vlaminck tirelessly painted the city as a lover would paint a nude, attempting to capture her many moods. There were Monet's ethereal representations of Paris out-of-doors, compositions that gave the impression of a far-away, almost make-believe place. And it was Hemingway who kept the cafés alive with poignant stories that said more in silence than they did in words.

It is among these silences that any real exploration of the art of Thomas Pradzynski must begin. His uninhabited street scenes give viewers a chance to examine the life of this fascinating old city beyond the outward emotion of her people, behind the veneer of human occupation. He portrays Paris on a deeper, more romantic plane where his existence becomes one with his subject. It has been said that Paris is to art what the heart is to

Café a Bonaparte, Paris, 1914.

Café de la Paix, Paris, 1913.

man, the mechanism that provides a lifeblood to the body artistic, the sustaining force that enables its growth to continue. For Thomas, Paris is indisputably the soul of his art. More than a place or a city, the inseparable role of inspiration and subject are immediately evident in his work, and therein we discover the reason that it has become the enigmatic center of his paintings. Pradzynski's love for life, and casual never-too-serious outlook on his own existence have melded with the spirit of this city, instilling in him an admiration for his adopted home that is intuitively observed in each of his compositions.

How many before him have shared these emotions, gathering creative strength from this city, inhabiting locales famous for producing some of arts most well known personalities? While today many — not all — artists go to Paris simply because it is where artists go, the pioneers of art went with different and varied motives. Chagall, for instance, fled persecution in Russia for a chance to live in freedom, while Modigliani

sought in Paris relief from the somber, almost melancholy attitude that pervaded Italy during the late 19th century and the first part of the 20th century. For Pradzynski, it represents the wonderment of youth, the playful childhood memories of his past. Most have taken something from Paris, but Thomas Pradzynski has given something back, a gift more precious than a painting or a sculpture or anything material: he has given life where life is no more or is soon to be gone, in the splendid old buildings he preserves forever in his work. An entire architectural heritage is being destroyed in favor of so-called "urban renewal" projects; in fact, Montparnasse, formerly one of the two main artist's "strongholds" (the other being Montmartre), is virtually devoid of these old venerated structures which Thomas reveres.

For some, Paris was not the end but a means to artistic growth and enrichment. It is a statement of fact that the most influential of art's movements —at least during the 19th and 20th centuries —began in Paris. The Realist movement, led by Courbet, had its roots in this city. Piccasso and his contemporaries, among them Derain and Matisse, led the world into Abstractism. Reacting to romanticism and traditional academic approaches to art in the late 19th century, Renoir and Monet developed the first examples of Impressionism in their studios here. Countless other offshoots, including Neo-Impressionism, Post-Impressionism, Fauvism and many more saw their beginnings in Paris.

Or, perhaps, is it the tolerant nature of Paris that draws so many hopeful painters, sculptors, illustrators and the like? One need only read a biography of any great artist to understand that there is an unquestioning permissiveness in Paris, an atmosphere that indulges any form of creative expression, no matter how extreme. No matter the medium or the subject, the style or method, any avenue of artistic inventiveness could be explored without fear of repression or rejection.

Paris brings to mind the specter of starving, young, destitute artists struggling, living from meal to meal. Not all who sought

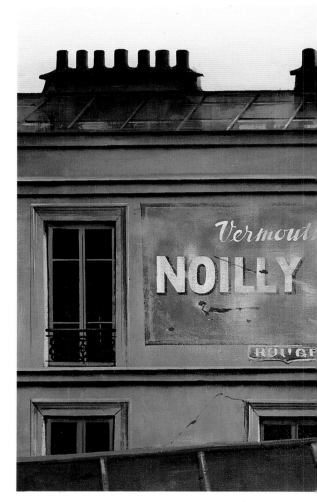

refuge here were poor: Gertrude Stein was from a family of substantial means and her brother, who introduced her to Picasso, had amassed a great collection of works while living in this bohemian setting. Others were not as fortunate. Thomas Pradzynski came to Paris under lesser circumstances — no job, little money and a dream of success. He, like

Noilly Prat

ACRYLIC ON CANVAS
45 X 106 CM. / 18 X 42 IN.
SIGNED: LOWER RIGHT
APRIL 1991

Marc Chagall and countless others, never lost sight of the goal, the dream; and as a result of that dedication, his career eventually flourished.

Paris has made Thomas Pradzynski a complete artist and he, in return, has made Paris his art. His paintings are visual poems, odes to a place only he has seen but one which he invites us to visit. It exists in silence, but resounds with the choruses of unseen life, cajoling us into singing along, seducing us into a world where reality and fantasy become a single entity. He celebrates the streets of this city, every window and doorway, every courtyard and cafe, he paints each as an exclamation of his love.

BELLE
ANS DU MARAIS
GALERIE
DU MIDI
LA BETE
PALAIS DE SPORT
CIRQUE
DUNLOP

95

The Graphic Works

A U G U S T   1 9 9 0   -   M A Y   1 9 9 4

Since the summer of 1990, Caldwell-Snyder has been working closely with Thomas Pradzynski and selected studios in developing special printmaking techniques that would best reflect the artist's style in limited edition graphics. The four participating studios, Kato Studio, Clearwater Studio, SOMA Fine Art Press and Morosstudio Inc., have all revealed for the artist numerous possibilities for his prints. Ultimately, after printing over thirty graphic editions, the artist and his collaborating printmakers have achieved a refined interpretation of his imagery into serigraphy.

Leonora

SERIGRAPH
AUGUST 1990

LEONORA

Boulangerie No. 28

LES MEMOIRES DE PARIS SUITE
SERIGRAPH
NOVEMBER 1990

BOULANGERIE No. 28

Rue du Porche

LES MEMOIRES DE PARIS SUITE
SERIGRAPH
NOVEMBER 1990

Serge Caillaud

LES MEMOIRES DE PARIS SUITE
SERIGRAPH
NOVEMBER 1990

L' Écluse Bar À Vin

BALLADES PARISIENNES SUITE
SERIGRAPH
JANUARY 1991

Le Caveau du Palais

BALLADES PARISIENNES SUITE
SERIGRAPH
JANUARY 1991

LE CAVEAU DU PALAIS

*Une Bicyclette
A Florence*

SERIGRAPH
MARCH 1991

UNE BICYCLETTE A FLORENCE

Antiquités

LA PETITE SUITE
SERIGRAPH
MAY 1991

Bicyclette Pl. Dauphine

La Petite Suite
SERIGRAPH
MAY 1991

Fenêtre No. 73

LA PETITE SUITE
SERIGRAPH
MAY 1991

F E N Ê T R E   N O .   7 3

Le Café

LA PETITE SUITE
SERIGRAPH
MAY 1991

LE CAFÉ

Librairie

LA PETITE SUITE
SERIGRAPH
MAY 1991

LIBRAIRIE

Le Bacchus Gourmand

SERIGRAPH
OCTOBER 1991

LE BACCHUS GOURMAND

Rear Window
———————————

SERIGRAPH
JANUARY 1992

REAR WINDOW

Twilight on Rue de

Madiran

SERIGRAPH
MARCH 1992

TWILIGHT ON RUE DE MADIRAN

Atelier de Gravure

LA MINIATURE SUITE
SERIGRAPH
JUNE 1992

La Place Dauphine

LA MINIATURE SUITE
SERIGRAPH
JUNE 1992

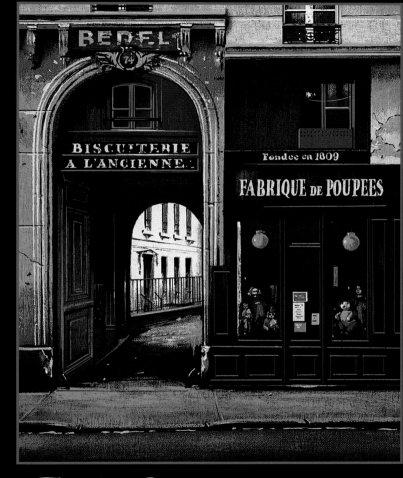

Fabrique de Poupées

La Grande Arche

SERIGRAPH
SEPTEMBER 1992

LA GRANDE ARCHE

Caves de France

SERIGRAPH
DECEMBER 1992

CAVES DE FRANCE

Atelier de Poterie

LA PETITE SUITE II
SERIGRAPH
MARCH 1993

ATELIER DE POTERIE

Cordonnerie

LA PETITE SUITE II
SERIGRAPH
MARCH 1993

La Bicyclette Rouge

LA PETITE SUITE II
SERIGRAPH
MARCH 1993

La Bicyclette Rouge

Marchand de Vin

La Petite Suite II
Serigraph
March 1993

MARCHAND DE VIN

Passage Delaunay

LA PETITE SUITE II
SERIGRAPH
MARCH 1993

PASSAGE DELAUNAY

Passage Molière

SERIGRAPH
MAY 1993

PASSAGE MOLIERE

Café de Paris

SERIGRAPH
JULY 1993

CAFÉ DE PARIS

Boulangerie No. 39

LES PROMENADES
PARISIENNES SUITE
SERIGRAPH
SEPTEMBER 1993

La Patisserie du Parc

LES PROMENADES
PARISIENNES SUITE
SERIGRAPH
SEPTEMBER 1993

Le Chat

LES PROMENADES
PARISIENNES SUITE
SERIGRAPH
SEPTEMBER 1993

Passage du Cheval Blanc

SERIGRAPH
DECEMBER 1993

PASSAGE DU CHEVAL BLANC

Galerie du Midi

THE COLLECTOR'S
BOOK EDITION I
SERIGRAPH
JANUARY 1994

Le Bistrot

THE COLLECTOR'S
BOOK EDITION II
SERIGRAPH
JANUARY 1994

Librairie St. Germain

THE COLLECTOR'S
BOOK EDITION III
SERIGRAPH
JANUARY 1994

Passage du Lyon d'Or

SERIGRAPH
JANUARY 1994

PASSAGE DU LYON D'OR

Garage St. Antoine

SERIGRAPH
MARCH 1994

GARAGE ST. ANTOINE

Artisans du Marais

SERIGRAPH
MAY 1994

ARTISANS DU MARAIS

Catalogue Raisonné

AUGUST 1990 - MAY 1994

The Catalogue Raisonné is a chronological listing of each edition, including applicable suite references, completion dates, print studios, disclosure information and any relevant data of interest to collectors, gallerists, museum curators and art historians. It includes all of Thomas Pradzynski's work published by Caldwell-Snyder Publishing from August 1990 through May 1994.

The staff at Caldwell-Snyder Publishing has made every effort possible in verifying the accuracy of the Catalogue Raisonné. A glossary of terms and definitions used in the Catalogue Raisonné is included. The last four paintings illustrated in this book will be made into serigraphs; Passage du Lyon d'Or, Garage St. Antoine, Artisans du Marais and Passage du Cheval Blanc.

Leonora

Publishing Date: August 1990
Atelier: Kato Studio
Paper size: 19 13/16" x 25 13/16"
Image size: 15" x 21 3/4"

Regular Edition printed on White Coventry Rag Paper.
1/250-250/250
AP 1/25-25/25
PP 1/5-5/5
HC 1/5-5/5

Deluxe Edition printed on Black Arches Paper.
1/100-100/100
AP 1/25-25/25
PP NONE
HC 1/5-5/5

Printer's chop mark on the lower left corner.

Boulangerie No. 28

Suite title: Les Memoires de Paris Suite
Publishing Date: November 1990
Atelier: Kato Studio
Paper size: 23 5/8" x 29 7/8"
Image size: 17 9/16" x 23 7/8"

Regular Edition printed on White Coventry Rag Paper.
1/250-250/250
AP 1/35-35/35
PP 1/5-5/5
HC 1/5-5/5

Deluxe Edition printed on Black Arches Paper.
1/100-100/100
AP 1/15-15/15
PP NONE
HC 1/10-10/10

Printer's chop mark on the lower left corner and Publisher's
chop mark on the lower right corner.

Rue du Porche

Suite title: Les Memoires de Paris Suite
Publishing Date: November 1990
Atelier: Kato Studio
Paper size: 23 13/16" x 29 7/8"
Image size: 17 3/4" x 24"

Regular Edition printed on White Coventry Rag Paper.
1/250-250/250
AP 1/35-35/35
PP 1/5-5/5
HC 1/5-5/5

Deluxe Edition printed on Black Arches Paper.
1/100-100/100
AP 1/15-15/15
PP NONE
HC 1/10-10/10

Printer's chop mark on the lower left corner and Publisher's
chop mark on the lower right corner.

Le Pave de la Tournelle

Suite title: Les Memoires de Paris Suite
Publishing Date: November 1990
Atelier: Kato Studio
Paper size: 23 11/16" x 30"
Image size: 18" x 24 1/4"

Regular Edition printed on White Coventry Rag Paper.
1/250-250/250
AP 1/35-35/35
PP 1/5-5/5
HC 1/5-5/5

Deluxe Edition printed on Black Arches Paper.
1/100-100/100
AP 1/15-15/15
PP NONE
HC 1/10-10/10

Printer's chop mark on the lower left corner and Publisher's
chop mark on the lower right corner.

Serge Caillaud

Suite title: Les Memoires de Paris Suite
Publishing Date: November 1990
Atelier: Kato Studio
Paper size: 23 5/8" x 29 7/8"
Image size: 17 3/4" x 24"

Regular Edition printed on White Coventry Rag Paper.
1/250-250/250
AP 1/35-35/35
PP 1/5-5/5
HC 1/5-5/5

Deluxe Edition printed on Black Arches Paper.
1/100-100/100
AP 1/15-15/15
PP NONE
HC 1/10-10/10

Printer's chop mark on the lower left corner and Publisher's
chop mark on the lower right corner.

L'Ecluse Bar A Vin

Suite title: Ballades Parisiennes Suite
Publishing Date: January 1991
Atelier: Kato Studio
Paper size: 29 13/16" x 23 11/16"
Image size: 23 15/16" x 17 3/4"

Regular Edition printed on White Coventry Rag Paper.
1/200-200/200
AP 1/25-25/25
PP 1/5-5/5
HC 1/9-9/9

Deluxe Edition printed on Black Arches Paper.
1/150-150/150
AP 1/25-25/25
PP NONE
HC 1/6-6/6

Printer's chop mark on the lower left corner and Publisher's chop mark on the lower right corner.

Le Caveau du Palais

Suite title: Ballades Parisiennes Suite
Publishing Date: January 1991
Atelier: Kato Studio
Paper size: 30 1/16" x 23 13/16"
Image size: 24 1/16" x 17 15/16"

Regular Edition printed on White Coventry Rag Paper.
1/200-200/200
AP 1/25-25/25
PP 1/5-5/5
HC 1/5-5/5

Deluxe Edition printed on Black Arches Paper.
1/150-150/150
AP 1/25-25/25
PP NONE
HC NONE

Printer's chop mark on the lower left corner and Publisher's chop mark on the lower right corner.

Une Bicyclette A Florence

Publishing Date: March 1991
Atelier: Kato Studio
Paper size: 34" x 26 7/8"
Image size: 28 1/2" x 21"

Regular Edition printed on White Coventry Rag Paper.
1/200-200/200
AP 1/25-25/25
PP 1/5-5/5
HC 1/10-10/10

Deluxe Edition printed on Black Arches Paper.
1/150-150/150
AP 1/25-25/25
PP NONE
HC 1/10-10/10

Printer's chop mark on the lower left corner and Publisher's chop mark on the lower right corner.

Antiquites

Suite title: La Petite Suite
Publishing Date: May 1991
Atelier: Clearwater Studios
Paper size: 22 9/16" x 19 1/8"
Image size: 16 1/16" x 13 1/16"

Regular Edition printed on White Westwind Paper.
1/200-200/200
AP 1/25-25/25
PP 1/5-5/5

Deluxe Edition printed on Black 2 Ply Museum Board.
1/150-150/150
AP 1/25-25/25
PP 1/5-5/5

Printer's chop mark on the lower left corner and Publisher's chop mark on the lower right corner.

Bicyclette Pl. Dauphine

Suite title: La Petite Suite
Publishing Date: May 1991
Atelier: Clearwater Studios
Paper size: 22 9/16" x 19 1/8"
Image size: 16" x 13"

Regular Edition printed on White Westwind Paper.
1/200-200/200
AP 1/25-25/25
PP 1/5-5/5

Deluxe Edition printed on Black 2 Ply Museum Board.
1/150-150/150
AP 1/25-25/25
PP 1/5-5/5

Printer's chop mark on the lower left corner and Publisher's chop mark on the lower right corner.

Fenêtre No. 73

Suite title: La Petite Suite
Publishing Date: May 1991
Atelier: Clearwater Studios
Paper size: 22 9/16" x 19 1/8"
Image size: 16 1/16" x 13"

Regular Edition printed on White Westwind Paper.
1/200-200/200
AP 1/25-25/25
PP 1/5-5/5

Deluxe Edition printed on Black 2 Ply Museum Board.
1/150-150/150
AP 1/25-25/25
PP 1/5-5/5

Printer's chop mark on the lower left corner and Publisher's chop mark on the lower right corner.

Le Café

Suite title: La Petite Suite
Publishing Date: May 1991
Atelier: Clearwater Studios
Paper size: 22 9/16" x 19 1/16"
Image size: 16 1/16" x 13 1/16"

Regular Edition printed on White Westwind Paper.
1/200-200/200
AP 1/25-25/25
PP 1/5-5/5

Deluxe Edition printed on Black 2 Ply Museum Board.
1/150-150/150
AP 1/25-25/25
PP 1/5-5/5

Printer's chop mark on the lower left corner and Publisher's chop mark on the lower right corner.

Librairie

Suite title: La Petite Suite
Publishing Date: May 1991
Atelier: Clearwater Studios
Paper size: 22 9/16" x 19 1/8"
Image size: 16 1/16" x 13 1/16"

Regular Edition printed on White Westwind Paper.
1/200-200/200
AP 1/25-25/25
PP 1/5-5/5
HC NONE

Deluxe Edition printed on Black 2 Ply Museum Board.
1/150-150/150
AP 1/25-25/25
PP 1/5-5/5

Printer's chop mark on the lower left corner and Publisher's chop mark on the lower right corner.

Le Bacchus Gourmand

Publishing Date: October 1991
Atelier: Clearwater Studios
Paper size: 35 3/8" x 45"
Image size: 28 7/8" x 38 15/16"

Regular Edition printed on White Westwind Paper.
1/200-200/200
AP 1/25-25/25
PP 1/5-5/5

Deluxe Edition printed on Black 2 Ply Museum Board.
1/150-150/150
AP 1/25-25/25
PP 1/5-5/5

Printer's chop mark on the lower left corner and Publisher's chop mark on the lower right corner.

Rear Window

Publishing Date: January 1992
Atelier: Clearwater Studios
Paper size: 30 11/16" x 23 15/16"
Image size: 24 3/16" x 17 15/16"

Regular Edition printed on White Westwind Paper.
1/200-200/200
AP 1/25-25/25
PP 1/5-5/5

Deluxe Edition printed on Black 2 Ply Museum Board.
1/150-150/150
AP 1/25-25/25
PP 1/5-5/5

Printer's chop mark on the lower left corner and Publisher's chop mark on the lower right corner.

Twilight on Rue de Madiran

Publishing Date: March 1992
Atelier: Clearwater Studios
Paper size: 24 9/16" x 47 1/2"
Image size: 18 1/16" x 41 7/16"

Regular Edition printed on White Westwind Paper.
1/200-200/200
AP 1/25-25/25
PP 1/5-5/5

Deluxe Edition printed on Black 2 Ply Museum Board.
1/150-150/150
AP 1/25-25/25
PP 1/5-5/5

Publisher's chop mark on the lower right corner.

Atelier de Gravure

Suite title: La Miniature Suite
Publishing Date: June 1992
Atelier: Clearwater Studios
Paper size: 17 1/8" x 14 5/8"
Image size: 10 1/2" x 8 1/2"

Regular Edition printed on White Museum Board.
1/200-200/200
AP 1/25-25/25
PP 1/5-5/5

Deluxe Edition printed on Black Museum Board.
1/150-150/150
AP 1/25-25/25
PP 1/5-5/5

Publisher's chop mark on the lower right corner.

Fabrique de Poupees

Suite title: La Miniature Suite
Publishing Date: June 1992
Atelier: Clearwater Studios
Paper size: 17 1/8" x 14 5/8"
Image size: 10 1/2" x 8 1/2"

Regular Edition printed on White Museum Board.
1/200-200/200
AP 1/25-25/25
PP 1/5-5/5

Deluxe Edition printed on Black Museum Board.
1/150-150/150
AP 1/25-25/25
PP 1/5-5/5

Publisher's chop mark on the lower right corner.

La Place Dauphine

Suite title: La Miniature Suite
Publishing Date: June 1992
Atelier: Clearwater Studios
Paper size: 17" x 21 9/16"
Image size: 10 1/2" x 15 1/2"

Regular Edition printed on White Museum Board.
1/200-200/200
AP 1/25-25/25
PP 1/5-5/5

Deluxe Edition printed on Black Museum Board.
1/150-150/150
AP 1/25-25/25
PP 1/5-5/5

Publisher's chop mark on the lower right corner.

La Grande Arche

Publishing Date: September 1992
Atelier: SOMA Fine Art Press
Paper size: 51 15/16" x 41"
Image size: 45 9/16" x 35 1/16"

Regular Edition printed on White Westwind Paper.
1/200-200/200
AP 1/25-25/25
PP 1/5-5/5

Deluxe Edition printed on Black Westwind Paper.
1/150-150/150
AP 1/25-25/25
PP 1/5-5/5

Printer's and Publisher's chop marks on the lower right corner.

Caves de France

Publishing Date: December 1992
Atelier: SOMA Fine Art Press
Paper size: 22 1/4" x 46"
Image size: 17 7/8" x 41 3/16"

Regular Edition printed on White Westwind Paper.
1/200-200/200
AP 1/25-25/25
PP 1/5-5/5

Deluxe Edition printed on Black Westwind Paper.
1/150-150/150
AP 1/25-25/25
PP 1/5-5/5

Printer's and Publisher's chop marks on the lower right corner.

Atelier de Poterie

Suite title: La Petite Suite II
Publishing Date: March 1993
Atelier: SOMA Fine Art Press
Paper size: 22 7/16" x 18 15/16"
Image size: 16 1/16" x 12 15/16"

Regular Edition printed on White Westwind Paper.
1/200-200/200
AP 1/25-25/25
PP 1/5-5/5

Deluxe Edition printed on Black Westwind Paper.
1/150-150/150
AP 1/25-25/25
PP 1/5-5/5

Printer's and Publisher's chop marks on the lower right corner.

Cordonnerie

Suite title: La Petite Suite II
Publishing Date: March 1993
Atelier: SOMA Fine Art Press
Paper size: 22 7/16" x 18 15/16"
Image size: 16 1/16" x 12 7/8"

Regular Edition printed on White Westwind paper.
1/200-200/200
AP 1/25-25/25
PP 1/5-5/5

Deluxe Edition printed on Black Westwind paper.
1/150-150/150
AP 1/25-25/25
PP 1/5-5/5

Printer's and Publisher's chop marks on the lower right corner.

La Bicyclette Rouge

Suite title: La Petite Suite II
Publishing Date: March 1993
Atelier: SOMA Fine Art Press
Paper size: 22 7/16" x 18 15/16"
Image size: 16 1/16" x 12 7/8"

Regular Edition printed on White Westwind Paper.
1/200-200/200
AP 1/25-25/25
PP 1/5-5/5

Deluxe Edition printed on Black Westwind Paper.
1/150-150/150
AP 1/25-25/25
PP 1/5-5/5

Printer's and Publisher's chop marks on the lower right corner.

Marchand de Vin

Suite title: La Petite Suite II
Publishing Date: March 1993
Atelier: SOMA Fine Art Press
Paper size: 22 7/16" x 19"
Image size: 16" x 12 7/8"

Regular Edition printed on White Westwind Paper.
1/200-200/200
AP 1/25-25/25
PP 1/5-5/5

Regular Edition printed on Black Westwind Paper.
1/150-150/150
AP 1/25-25/25
PP 1/5-5/5

Printer's and Publisher's chop marks on the lower right corner.

Passage Delaunay

Suite title: La Petite Suite II
Publishing Date: March 1993
Atelier: SOMA Fine Art Press
Paper size: 22 7/16" x 18 15/16"
Image size: 16 1/16" x 12 7/8"

Regular Edition printed on White Westwind Paper.
1/200-200/200
AP 1/25-25/25
PP 1/5-5/5

Deluxe Edition printed on Black Westwind Paper.
1/150-150/150
AP 1/25-25/25
PP 1/5-5/5

Printer's and Publisher's chop marks on the lower right corner.

Passage Moliere

Publishing Date: May 1993
Atelier: SOMA Fine Art Press
Paper size: 24 1/2" x 47 3/4"
Image size: 18" x 41 11/16"

Regular Edition printed on White Coventry Rag Paper.
1/200-200/200
AP 1/25-25/25
PP 1/5-5/5

Deluxe Edition printed on Black Arches Paper.
1/150-150/150
AP 1/25-25/25
PP 1/5-5/5

Printer's and Publisher's chop marks on the lower right corner.

Café de Paris

Publishing Date: July 1993
Atelier: SOMA Fine Art Press
Paper size: 27 9/16" x 51 1/2"
Image size: 21 1/8" x 45 1/2"

Regular Edition printed on White Coventry Rag Paper.
1/200-200/200
AP 1/25-25/25
PP 1/5-5/5

Deluxe Edition printed on Black Arches Paper.
1/150-150/150
AP 1/25-25/25
PP 1/5-5/5

Printer's and Publisher's chop marks on the lower right corner.

Boulangerie No. 39

Suite title: Les Promenades Parisiennes Suite
Publishing Date: October 1993
Atelier: Morosstudio, Inc.
Paper size: 17 1/4" x 14 1/4"
Image size: 10 3/4" x 8 1/4"

Regular Edition printed on White Coventry Rag Paper.
1/200-200/200
AP 1/25-25/25
PP 1/3-3/3

Deluxe Edition printed on Black Arches Paper.
1/150-150/150
AP 1/25-25/25
PP 1/2-2/2

Publisher's chop mark on the lower right corner.

La Patisserie du Parc

Suite title: Les Promenades Parisiennes Suite
Publishing Date: October 1993
Atelier: Morosstudio, Inc.
Paper size: 17 1/4" x 21 1/2"
Image size: 10 3/4" x 15 1/2"

Regular Edition printed on White Coventry Rag Paper.
1/200-200/200
AP 1/25-25/25
PP 1/3-3/3

Deluxe Edition printed on Black Arches Paper.
1/150-150/150
AP 1/25-25/25
PP 1/2-2/2

Publisher's chop mark on the lower right corner.

Le Chat

Suite title: Les Promenades Parisiennes Suite
Publishing Date: October 1993
Atelier: Morosstudio, Inc.
Paper size: 17 1/4" x 14 1/4"
Image size: 10 3/4" x 8 1/4"

Regular Edition printed on White Coventry Rag Paper.
1/200-200/200
AP 1/25-25/25
PP 1/3-3/3

Deluxe Edition printed on Black Arches Paper.
1/150-150/150
AP 1/25-25/25
PP 1/2-2/2

Publisher's chop mark on the lower right corner.

Passage du Cheval Blanc

Publishing Date: December 1993
Atelier: Morosstudio, Inc.
Paper size: 24 1/2" x 47 1/2"
Image size: 18" x 41 1/2"

Regular Edition printed on White Coventry Rag Paper.
1/200-200/200
AP 1/25-25/25
PP 1/3-3/3

Deluxe Edition printed on Black Arches Paper.
1/150-150/150
AP 1/25-25/25
PP 1/2-2/2

Publisher's chop mark on the lower right corner.

Galerie du Midi

Series title: Collector's Edition I
Publishing Date: January 1994
Atelier: Morosstudio, Inc.
Paper size: 12 1/4" x 9 3/4"
Image size: 8 3/4" x 6 3/4"

Regular Edition printed on White Coventry Rag Paper.
1/200-200/200
AP 1/25-25/25
PP 1/3-3/3

Deluxe Edition printed on Black Arches Paper.
1/150-150/150
AP 1/25-25/25
PP 1/2-2/2

Publisher's chop mark on the lower right corner.

Le Bistrot

Series title: Collector's Edition II
Publishing Date: January 1994
Atelier: Morosstudio, Inc.
Paper size: 12 1/4" x 9 3/4"
Image size: 8 3/4" x 6 3/4"

Regular Edition printed on White Coventry Rag Paper.
1/200-200/200
AP 1/25-25/25
PP 1/3-3/3

Deluxe Edition printed on Black Arches Paper.
1/150-150/150
AP 1/25-25/25
PP 1/2-2/2

Publisher's chop mark on the lower right corner.

Librairie St. Germain

Series title: Collector's Edition III
Publishing Date: January 1994
Atelier: Morosstudio, Inc.
Paper size: 12 1/4" x 9 3/4"
Image size: 8 3/4" x 6 3/4"

Regular Edition printed on White Coventry Rag Paper.
1/200-200/200
AP 1/25-25/25
PP 1/3-3/3

Deluxe Edition printed on Black Arches Paper.
1/150-150/150
AP 1/25-25/25
PP 1/2-2/2

Publisher's chop mark on the lower right corner.

Passage du Lyon d'Or

Publishing Date: January 1994
Atelier: Morosstudio, Inc.
Paper size: 52" x 41"
Image size: 45 1/2" x 35"

Regular Edition printed on White Coventry Rag Paper.
1/200-200/200
AP 1/25-25/25
PP 1/3-3/3

Deluxe Edition printed on Black Arches Paper.
1/150-150/150
AP 1/25-25/25
PP 1/2-2/2

Publisher's chop mark on the lower right corner.

Garage St. Antoine

Publishing Date: March 1994
Atelier: Morosstudio, Inc.
Paper size: 32" x 45"
Image size: 25 1/2" x 39"

Regular Edition printed on White Coventry Rag paper.
1/200-200/200
AP 1/25-25/25
PP 1/3-3/3

Deluxe Edition printed on Black Arches Paper.
1/150-150/150
AP 1/25-25/25
PP 1/2-2/2

Publisher's chop mark on the lower right corner.

Artisans du Marais

Publishing Date: May 1994
Atelier: Morosstudio, Inc.
Paper size: 29 1/4" x 51 1/2"
Image size: 22 3/4" x 45 1/2"

Regular Edition printed on White Coventry Rag Paper.
1/200-200/200
AP 1/25-25/25
PP 1/3-3/3

Deluxe Edition printed on Black Arches Paper.
1/150-150/150
AP 1/25-25/25
PP 1/2-2/2

Publisher's chop mark on the lower right corner.

Print Index

Glossary

Edition: The number of prints pulled, numbered and signed by the artist. Each edition may consist of Arabic numbered impressions, artist's proofs, hors commerce proofs, printer's proofs, trial proofs, presentation proofs, or any combination thereof. The denominator (lower number) indicates the size of the edition, the numerator (upper number) the sequence in which the impressions were signed. The Arabic numbered impressions are signed by the artist and consecutively numbered (e.g., 1/150, 2/150, 3/150 . . . 150/150). The artist's proofs (AP) are impressions outside the Arabic numbered edition, are signed by the artist and consecutively numbered (e.g., AP 1/25, AP 2/25 . . . AP 25/25). The printer's proofs (PP) are impressions outside the Arabic numbered edition, are signed by the artist and consecutively numbered (e.g., PP 1/5, 2/5 . . . PP5/5). They are usually reserved for the printers. Presentation proofs and/or trial proofs are impressions outside the numbered edition and used by the publisher as presentation examples for the trade. Hors Commerce proofs are impressions outside the Arabic numbered edition, are signed by the artist and consecutively numbered (e.g., HC 1/10, 2/10, . . . 10/10). They are usually reserved for the publisher.

Chop Mark: The personal embossed seal of the publisher and/or collaborating printer of the edition. When this chop mark or embossed seal is used, it is usually at the bottom of each impression and will appear on every signed impression in the edition.

Serigraphy: One of the four major divisions of fine art printmaking; commonly referred to as silk-screen printing. A serigraph print is made by a stencil technique using fabric (silk or synthetic) stretched tightly over a frame. The nonprinting areas on the fabric are blocked out by adhering a stencil. The image areas are porous fabric which ink or paint is forced through with a squeegee. The paper to be printed is placed on the table , the screen is placed on top, ink is applied through the screen openings directly to the paper. The name "serigraph" was coined in the United States for silkscreen prints made in the late 1930's. Anthony Velonis, credited for the name and much of the new interest in the medium, was a painter, graphic designer and the leader of the federally sponsored art project for screen printing under the Works Project Administration (WPA).

Bibliography

BIBLIOGRAPHY

Bibliography

Houghton Mifflin Company *1993 Information Please Almanac* 1992, Houghton Mifflin Company

Hughes, Robert *Shock of the New* 1981, Alfred Knopf

Janson, H. W. *History of Art* 1974, Harry N. Abrams Publishers

Kagan, Andrew *Chagall* 1989, Cross River Press Limited

Kluver, John & Martin, Julie *Ki Ki's Paris* 1989, Harry N. Abrams Publishers

Levin, Gail *Edward Hopper, The Art and the Artist* 1980, Norton / Whitney Museum

Lieberman, William S. *Pablo Picasso* 1954, Harry N. Adams, Incorporated

Milner, John *The Studios of Paris* 1988, Yale University Press

Nochlin, Linda *Realism* 1971, Hartmansworth, Penguin

Perl, Jed *Paris without End: On French Art since World War I* 1988, North Point Press

Roy, Claude *Modigliani* 1958, Editions d'Art Albert Skira

Takashin, Shji *Paris in Japan* 1987, Japan Foundation

175

une **ABSINTHE**
EDOUARD PERNOD
PONTARLIER

Maison fondée en 1827

GAZ
A TOUT LES ETAGES

15

SEMELLES
Reparations

L.DUVAL
PHOTOGRAPHE

GRAMOPHONES

D. Lenoir

TSF